MY SIDE OF THE STREET

MY SIDE OF
THE STREET

Why Wolves,
Flash Boys, Quants, and
Masters of the Universe
Don't Represent the Real
Wall Street

Jason DeSena Trennert

St. Martin's Press ⚜ New York

www.stmartins.com

Designed by Patrice Sheridan

The Library of Congress Cataloging-in-Publication Data is available upon request.

ISBN 978-1-250-06827-9 (hardcover)
ISBN 978-1-4668-7715-3 (e-book)

St. Martin's Press books may be purchased for educational, business, or promotional use. For information on bulk purchases, please contact the Macmillan Corporate and Premium Sales Department at 1-800-221-7945, extension 5442, or write to specialmarkets@ macmillan.com.

First Edition: May 2015

10 9 8 7 6 5 4 3 2 1

To Bev,

for putting up with my vanities, insecurities,
ambitions, and all their attendant anxieties

CONTENTS

"Is not commercial credit based primarily upon money or property?"

"No, sir," replied J. P. Morgan. "The first thing is character."

"Before money or property?"

"Before money or anything else. Money cannot buy it . . . Because a man I do not trust could not get money from me on all the bonds in Christendom."

—J. P. MORGAN,
responding to lead prosecutor Samuel Untermyer at the
Pujo hearings investigating the "money trust" in front of
the House Committee on Banking and Currency

The world breaks everyone and afterward many are strong in the broken places.

—ERNEST HEMINGWAY,
A Farewell to Arms

PREFACE

One of the more famous *New Yorker* cartoons depicts an idiot king slouched and drooling on his throne in the foreground, while in the background one palace guard says to another, "It's either this or a government run by lawyers." As it is with democracy, so it is with free markets and the engine that makes them run—Wall Street. Any system based on a freedom to choose will, almost by definition, be at times unsightly and inefficient. Still, it raises the question: what's the alternative? Many other more autocratic systems have been attempted but they all inevitably lead to greater and more pernicious inequities—the very things they were designed to prevent. Wall Street, despite all its blemishes, provides a vital function in a free society: it breathes life into the dreams of everyday people, from a quirky guy building a business in a garage in Silicon Valley to a middle-class kid from Long Island with no connections.

MY SIDE OF THE STREET

NIGHTS AT ROTHMANN'S

There exists in Midtown Manhattan a little street that could, until recently, tell you more about what's happening in the world of finance in an hour than you could find out at the corner of Broad and Wall in a whole day. In the context of this great metropolis, there is nothing particularly special about Fifty-fourth Street between Madison and Fifth. There's a deli on the corner that sells just about everything known to man and where people buy their lunch by the pound. There's a shoe store across the street and a beautiful neoclassical building down the block that houses perhaps the best and most expensive men's clothing store in the city. But what made this particular street important as far as Wall Street is concerned were two restaurants that sat across the street from each other: San Pietro, an elite Italian bistro on the south side, and Rothmann's, a steak house on the north side. The prices of the restaurants weren't all that different; each catered to expense account honchos not paying with their own money. Yet the seventy-five feet of asphalt separating these two establishments might as well be the difference between Athens and Marathon. San Pietro is a bastion of the market's chess masters; Rothmann's, which closed last summer, of its well-polished pawns.

As a denizen of New York and a Wall Streeter through and through, I have spent considerable time in both establishments. To be honest, I am a visitor in one and was a tribe member in the other. I make my pilgrimage to San Pietro once a month to see the "masters of the universe" the same way others might visit a zoo. I have tried in vain on two occasions to become a regular there. On the first I used my dining companion, a Wall Street strategist of considerable fame. On the second I used my Neapolitan roots. Neither worked. Both were greeted with a wan smile that said, "Nice try, *uaglio,* but you're about twenty years and nine figures short."

And so, as is the case with just about every other place that caters to people who take themselves too seriously in this city, I have been relegated to the role of visitor and go instead with my friend Charlie, who has carved out what seems to be a firmly cemented status as the journalist who knows more about what's under the fingernails of the financial industry than anyone else. And he spots the dirt instantly, even here, a place I viewed as hallowed ground, the sanctum sanctorum of modern financial titans.

"You see Mack and Fink over there?" he might observe excitedly. "They're probably talking about how to split up the world between them!" Then he checks his BlackBerry nervously before scanning for other stars: "That's Greenhill. And there's Langone and Perella!" He tries to whisper but in his excitement ends up nearly shouting. "The guy who runs Guggenheim," he blurts, while nodding toward another table. "What's his name?" He checks his BlackBerry again, not waiting for an answer, before we resume our typically desultory conversation about the latest dramas in a business that has become a spectacle all by itself. Lunch with Charlie is always fun, but exhausting.

Such is San Pietro's, a canteen of sorts for the city's financial elite. The rest of us felt more comfortable across the street tucked into Rothmann's. We're the rank and file securities analysts, the traders, and the salesmen; in truth, we're all salesmen. We're all brokers of one sort or another and we talk about what most men in their thirties and forties talk about in this business: golf, the markets, office politics, and women. I felt so comfortable in this place that I counted its maître d', Pat Feliti, as a part of my extended family on the Street. He's the type of guy who would, in a pinch, let you sleep in the storeroom if your wife threw you out.

Rothmann's was by no means cheap—a martini would still cost you fourteen dollars—but it was hard to feel insecure there. During the salad days before the financial crisis, a group of us had assembled at the bar every Thursday pretty much since it opened its doors for business in 1999. We are a dog's breakfast of Wall Street personalities. There's Jimmy who uses "the box" and dark pools and IM—the electronic forms of trading that have largely replaced the need to speak directly to other human beings—the way guys of a different era used a pick and shovel. He likes the business well enough but prefers to talk about sports and "broads." If he beats the VWAP (a basic measure of trading efficiency) and takes clients out a few times a week, his manager is happy and can sleep the sleep of the just. "In the midst of all this," he says sardonically, "our cents per share has gone up to 4.6. I'm half expecting the sun to set in the East and the birds to fly north for the winter."

And then there's Billy, an irrepressibly likable and fun guy with a head as big as a stop sign who couldn't tell you where the S&P is trading on any given day if you put a gun to his head. He's hit the jackpot with this job as an institutional salesman and, at age forty-three, can afford to count among his dependents two wives, three vacation properties, and two bartenders. Billy's never been pretentious enough to believe he could provide the financial perspicacity of Bernard Baruch, but he can sure get you what you want—access to the firm's top research analysts, suitable allocations of hot IPOs, a seat at the firm's conference for top clients— all while using his expense account to keep you happy, entertained, and well fed. He is, in this way, a master of what's becoming a lost art.

Then there's Brian, who works at a hedge fund and looks like he came straight out of Central Casting as an Ivy League fraternity brother from the fifties. He senses the great absurdities in this business—like the fact that the smartest people in the industry come close to torching the financial markets every ten years. He's also one of the funniest guys you've ever met.

Often at the edge of the our crowd, half sitting on a stool at the bar, was "Links," an irrepressibly funny ballbuster who had worked on the floor of the New York Stock Exchange since the late 1960s—when commissions were fixed, the job was fun and high paying, and the position carried with it some cache. "Read two papers a day—the *Daily Racing Form* and the *New York Post*," he'd advise us, and would also regale us with ridiculous stories, like the time he had Dick Grasso fetch him coffee. Not possessing a seat on the exchange, our firm hired Links, his son, and their eponymous firm as our representatives on the floor. (In a sign of just how much times had changed, such firms were still referred to colloquially as two-dollar brokers, a vestige of better days. Today, shares are transacted at fractions of a penny.) Links's son, Tommy, worked with him in what was supposed to be the family business. He played junior college football at a state school upstate and received an associate's degree in business administration. A moose of a guy with a kind heart, Tommy was destined to take over the business, as his father had begun to spend more time warming his aging bones with his friends on a golf course in Vero Beach. He was funny, too, and if he liked you or if you said something that made him laugh, he would slap you on the back so hard you'd lose your breath. Tommy was, quite literally, a backslapper. After the tech bubble burst in the early 2000s, Links started to look a little more drawn and tired. His standby Ferragamo loafers were replaced with sensible black, rubber-soled, lace-up shoes, his tie was a little looser than it used to be, and his signature pair of cuff links more predictable.

Rothmann's has been a great constant in the pageant of my life. Most of my great successes, defeats, sorrows, triumphs, and sins were either celebrated or mourned within its four walls. The pivotal decision to start my own firm resulted from one particularly long evening there. I was ensconced in my hangout trying to shake off one in what had become a series of frequent hangovers and to make sense of my life. It was 2005, and we on Wall Street were still blissfully unaware that a financial tsunami would crash over our lives within three short years. I loved the financial markets, had a great job, traveled the world, and had a beautiful family. Yet despite all this, dark questions about my future and my character plagued me: Who was I? Why did I have so much yet still feel miserable? Was I a phony? Did I drink too much? Why was I sometimes bitter?

Attempting to answer these questions, I came to the conclusion that a good part of my unhappiness stemmed from the fact that I missed my father, and saw little of his greatest virtue—an abiding commitment to being genuine—in myself or many of my colleagues. I was in my midthirties at the time and still holding on to the romantic and borderline-infantile belief that we on Wall Street were all in this thing together. The old-time investors who took their roles as fiduciaries of other people's money seriously were steadily being replaced by quick-buck artists who had little regard for the Street's traditions, its rhythms, or its broader role in society.

One particularly long night alone at the bar early in 2006 led me to map out my new path for my own firm on cocktail napkins. By September, my partners and I opened Strategas's doors.

Two years later, in the slow and glorious Christmas season of 2008, I decided to start the book you now hold in your hands. Bear Stearns had failed that spring, and by then, even the least introspective among us began to wonder whether our sense of the universe and our place within it had been irrevocably altered. The grand sense that we as Wall Street veterans were the lucky ones who could cheat the humdrum existence of executives in other industries started to fade. The mighty were falling. The conversations you'd hear at Rothmann's changed markedly. Now meant less to impress each other, they centered on trying to make sense of what was happening to our industry, our town, and our careers. Maybe, just maybe, we weren't all worth the lofty salaries and bonuses that accompanied even midlevel jobs in the finance industry.

That night, Billy was trying to get one of his big hedge fund clients, a long/short firm specializing in health care stocks, to do more business with his firm. He had invited one of his colleagues to join us, a new quantitative analyst—in the vernacular, a quant— on their desk named Omar. The feeling about quantitative analysts or quants—first hired by Salomon Brothers in the late 1980s— was that they could remove the inherent human biases of the old Wall Street through the bloodless application of mathematics. Old-fashioned virtues like prudence based on both instinct and experience were thought to be less efficient than the careful application of quantitative analysis to economic and financial data.

Very young and endowed with a newly minted degree in chemical engineering, Omar had graduated first in his class from a college in India that accepted only one in ten thousand applicants. He was alleged to be able to make an Excel spreadsheet sing.

Not knowing a lot about baseball or about the Masters, he was quiet at first. But once the conversation lurched inevitably toward the collapse of Bear and the demise of its honchos Jimmy Cayne and Warren Spector, he spat out, in an East Asian accent, "What the fuck is VAR anyway when you're leveraged thirty-three to one?"*

We all began to laugh at the unexpected bitterness emanating from this elegant young man. It was clear that Omar had been betrayed by youth and overconfidence in the power of math when it came to the prices of securities. He had never heard of Penn Central or Continental Illinois or Drexel Burnham, all firms that had failed despite—or perhaps because of—their great strength and sense of invincibility, and he didn't care to for that matter. He had come to America to make money, and the random events on a bell curve of possible outcomes that were rarely supposed to happen (so-called fat tails) were occurring with shocking regularity. The belief that finance could be a science unto itself, rather than a social science subject to the emotions of imperfect human beings, was screwing up his plan of instant riches.

His ire was amusing at first, but the laughter soon faded. Silence ensued as we again faced the fact that we all knew guys just like us who had lost their fortunes and were about to lose their jobs. In the years to come, the thousands of men and women who worked on the floor of the New York Stock Exchange would be replaced by computers, the venerated proprietary traders of the investment banks who were charged with trading the firm's own

---

* VAR is an acronym for value at risk, a popular financial formula that was putatively designed to alert the managements of investment banks as to just how much they were taking with their own trades and dealings with clients. Unfortunately, many forgot that financial models are only as good as the assumptions that underpin them. Events once thought to be impossible, like an overall decline in the value of real estate for instance, became shockingly possible.

money were to be regulated out of existence, and those of us who were once called customers' men were going to have to work harder to maintain lifestyles we had started to take for granted. The more introspective among us started to wonder whether we had traded our adult lives for free rounds of golf, unlimited use of the company's car service, and the shellfish tower at Smith & Wollensky's. The chasm between San Pietro and its financial virtuosos and the rest of us Wall Street journeymen at Rothmann's was getting wider.

After Lehman failed in September 2008, the tone and tenor of our conversations would change yet again. In much the same way it has been said that a recession occurs when a friend loses his job, but a depression occurs when you lose yours, we started to wonder whether there would be a place for us in what was certain to be a new and radically different global financial infrastructure. Lehman's failure led to existential questions about capitalism in general and Wall Street in particular. In those short days of autumn, no one was quite as sure as they had been of their abilities or their futures. The price of the stocks of investment banks, and as a result, the deferred compensation of thousands of Wall Street professionals, evaporated. I don't care how much money you have in the bank, no one can lose ten figures in company stock and not feel somewhat less sure of themselves. Only massive intervention from the Federal Reserve and the federal government could save the industry and, for that matter, the economy. Even the old-timers had no idea what the new capital markets would look like and what effect that might have on the broader economy and the great city that called it home, New York. Massive cash infusions saved the industry, but not before the receding tide of securities prices revealed more than the arrogance and recklessness of the industry's masters of the universe. Inevitably, what famed economist John Kenneth Galbraith called the bezzle—the hidden costs of greed in good times—becomes visible when times get tough.

It felt as though a significant number of Wall Street regulars began a great footrace to hit their "number" before their actual fair market value kicked in. They hoped the prevailing trade winds would sail them to a safe retirement harbor long before heavy weather forced them to change their plans. For financiers, the anxiety-provoking, existential crisis–producing questions came down to this: what was the real price of mediocrity when it had been overpriced for so long?

Did it matter that you had been a decent student and a great lacrosse player at Georgetown when budgets needed to be cut? Would your bosses care? Would your clients on the buy side? These kinds of questions pressed on us as the cost of everything tumbled back to earth and deflation set in. The prices of co-ops and 450 cc drivers plummeted, as did the fees for Pilates classes, and even the tuition for private schools. Men who previously thought themselves well on the way to being crowned masters of the universe began to take a much less optimistic view of the future.

One night, Jimmy looked at me across the bar and said, "Hey, Jase, you think you could interview my cousin for a job this summer? I've been telling him to get into research." He paused and looked wistfully into the bottom of an empty rocks glass. "I wouldn't wish the trading life on anybody these days," he continued, distrusting what many of us had spent our lives doing. "Research is safer. It's all about providing value now." When you're under fifty, it's unsettling to hear a guy who went to Duke talk about his chosen profession the way guys on the line talked about cars and steel a generation ago: as fading businesses.

I have known no other business than Wall Street since I started as a paid-by-the-hour cold caller at nineteen. So you can imagine how it pains me to read article after article characterizing Wall Street as made up solely of overpaid soulless overachievers who cheat and steal at the expense of "average" people. My pain stems from the belief that a career spent studying and interpreting the capital markets is an honorable one and that investing to benefit one's clients is admirable. I have known countless Wall Street professionals who take their roles as fiduciaries—as trusted agents with a moral responsibility to protect their clients—seriously. This is the nuance that the financial media has typically missed in reporting the market's troubles over the past six years, ridden with scandal as it has been. I realized just how low the reputation of the field had become on the sidelines of one of my son's lacrosse games last fall when another father and I started chatting about what we did for a living. When I told him that I worked at a brokerage firm his eyes lit up.

"Say, I just saw *The Wolf of Wall Street*. Wow! Was it really like that? Did you guys bring hookers up to the office and party like that? Incredible!"

"No. Really most people would think my job was pretty boring."

"Gee," he said, disappointed. "That's too bad."

"Yeah I guess so," I said laughing. "But think of it this way. You run a group of pharma sales reps, right?"

"Yeah."

"Well, from my perspective that has about as much in common with a what a drug dealer on the street corner does was with what *The Wolf of Wall Street* shows. They're really not alike at all aside from the fact that most of us are selling something."

Perhaps he was disappointed that there really were no parties with hookers or perhaps he had read one too many articles about the shabby behavior of "financiers." But I could tell my defense of my own profession did little to convince him. It wasn't long ago that a lot of men and women on Wall Street would be proud of their chosen profession. Now, a lot of us just want to change the subject.

But the thing you'll never see in the media is that the industry's scandals are perpetrated by a small minority. Scandal sells newspapers and magazines, but it doesn't begin to tell the whole story. In fact, not only does it fail to tell the whole story, but it also distorts and obscures the larger reality, which is this: most Wall Streeters are honest professionals, ethical and decent men and women.

That's what I'm writing this book to prove. And the stories told herein are all true, though in some cases I've taken poetic license to protect not only the innocent but also the not so innocent. This can be assumed in stories in which first names only are used. This memoir isn't meant to be a tell-all and it certainly is not intended to "get" or to hurt anyone. I am writing it simply to lighten the blackening effects of a frenzied and overboard media, to provide a few laughs for the reader, to supply a much-needed catharsis for the author, and, most important, to write out a prescription for the industry and our economy that might restore reputations lost and prestige tarnished.

I will cover the vast changes I've witnessed over three decades, a period in which technology has transformed almost every part of the business, from the simple matter of how trades are conducted and cleared to the skills needed to conduct them to the kinds of people who turn up for work each day. It's also a period in which increasingly elevated stakes attracted a new breed of Wall Streeter—hordes of guys with fancy degrees, bespoke suits, custom shirts, prescription-less tortoiseshell eyeglasses, and a penchant for activities like squash and running marathons simply for the fun of it. What's worse is many don't see the importance of their industry and tend to view their clients in "flyover" states as suckers rather than important partners. Watching them, I miss the guys they replaced: guys from the outer boroughs with thick New York accents, pinky rings, pastel short-sleeve dress shirts, and often atrocious eating and drinking habits.

Like it or not, New York has long been a company town, eclipsing London as the world's financial center when Britain's hegemonic influence declined and America's grew in the twentieth century. The growth of the financial services industry provided hundreds of thousands of well-paying jobs to men and women who were often the children of immigrants and not to the manor born. It gave regular people a chance to move into the upper middle class and, if they were lucky, the realm of the wealthy. The irony, of course, is that the financial crisis hurt the least culpable Wall Street workers the most. The captains of industry who created and presided over the "colossal failure of common sense" more or less wound up just fine, financially. It was the Wall Street working stiff who saw his earnings power fall most dramatically. In this way, Wall Street's connection with regular people has actually diminished rather than strengthened in the aftermath of the crash. That's progress, I guess, but it's a pity just the same.

Even as an undergraduate I enjoyed writing and planned to write as an adult in whatever career I pursued. Wall Street offers a glittering background and tumultuous stories. For years I toyed with the idea of writing the great American novel through the eyes of a Wall Streeter. I wanted as narrator an insider, a real participant, a veteran of the mad scrum, not a Nick Carraway type hanging on the fringes and idolizing Gatsby and the other giants of gainful trading. But fiction, even silly sensationalized stuff, is not as vivid and impactful as the real stories of Wall Street. They can rival any fiction in their potential to convey the great ironies of life. And then again, that book's been written before, many times over. And so I resolved to revise my vision.

A few years ago, I settled on writing a memoir, but I couldn't decide what sort of voice I could assume that might not only say something but also entertain the reader. My first iteration was a confessional sort of homage to Frederick Exley's stormy memoir,

A Fan's Notes, only featuring feisty financiers instead of professional football fanatics. Another New York City institution, Wall Street, would replace the New York Giants. This abandoned book would have explained the sins and struggles of financial professionals as the inevitable byproducts of the long hours, soul-crushing travel, and scads of money available. Ultimately, I found this angle too clichéd and realized that the book wouldn't be news to anyone who'd ever attended a bachelor party. Though I'm no saint, my own more traditional vices would never suffice for an entire book and would seriously undershoot the mark for a true exposé.

Briefly—very briefly—I also considered a revenge book, a kind of roman à clef, with thinly veiled characters and slightly altered real-life situations and historical scams. It would reveal the endless variety of phonies, charlatans, and talentless middle managers that too frequently occupy the ranks of corporate America in general and of Wall Street in particular. Here my own timidity and common sense quickly got the better of me. A hopelessly imperfect character myself, I feared I wouldn't be tough enough to withstand the blowback and that I might, metaphorically, find myself professionally isolated on my own self-made version of Elba. Discretion here would be the better part of valor.

The end result of all this creative speculation is the book that follows. It's a stream-of-consciousness account of my personal love affair with a greatly imperfect yet important industry. Like all great love affairs, my relationship with Wall Street excited my interests, passions, and ambitions, at times broke my heart, and occasionally tempted me to abandon a proletarian nature that prizes above all else a respect for fate. Mercifully, my ongoing affair with Wall Street hasn't paralleled Lampedusa's description of marriage in his great novel *The Leopard.* It hasn't been six weeks of ecstasy, the rest ashes. At least not yet it hasn't.

I'm writing this book for myself (and also for you, but mostly for me), prompted and sustained by requited love acquired and nourished on my three-decade journey down Wall Street. Knowing that *verbant volant, scriptet manent*, I'm putting this love letter into writing as a personal historical record so it will endure, outliving any fleeting television interview or blip of an op-ed squib. I did my best to banish investment bromides or financial clichés. Instead I want readers to know that it's a noble profession, why I think it has lost the public's trust, and how I know that trust can be regained. As Wordsworth said in his immortal ode, "Though nothing can bring back the hour of splendor in the grass, of glory in the flower, we will grieve not, rather find strength in what remains behind."

1

WELL, IT'S A START

Although I sought to go to the best schools, or at least the most prestigious ones, I have come to the conclusion that where one went to college is at best a poor predictor of future success, and at worst, completely inconsequential. When we seek to hire people for my company today, the quality of the college from which they graduated—or even if the candidate ever graduated from college—is *never* discussed. Life on Wall Street, mercifully, doesn't demand the kind of academic talent that might be required of a brain surgeon or an astrophysicist; it merely requires hustle, commercial aggressiveness, a genuine interest in the business, and—if one wants to stick around for a while—a sense of ethics and camaraderie that might help you survive the lean times.

But I didn't know any of this when I entered Georgetown University's School of Foreign Service in the fall of 1986 with the vague hope of becoming a foreign service officer or a CIA operative. It was exciting to be in Washington in the 1980s and my period of self-discovery was at times unsettling and painful. To the considerable consternation of my unionized public school teacher parents, I remained a Democrat for precisely one semester. The hurly-burly of then-mayor Marion Barry's Washington, DC, seemed so much more depressing and hopeless than President Reagan's view of America. Mayor Barry, I thought, saw the poor as a means to acquire political power, while Reagan saw poverty as a potentially temporary condition in a country built on the dignity of the individual. Georgetown's few rebels and revolutionaries seemed unnecessarily angry about the wrong things and were often spoiled kids who wouldn't ultimately have to worry all that much about getting jobs after graduation anyway.

My career ambitions shifted with my political beliefs. I soon realized that the chances of my cheerfully processing passport applications in Mali after graduation were zero. To start, I was too big a fan of Western civilization and, perhaps more important, I hated roughing it. As far as the CIA was concerned, I had virtually no ability to keep a secret, a serious liability for someone who was almost perpetually suntanned. I was never going to be the guy who could "blend."

Nowadays, it seems that most people anticipating a career in business line up a series of ever more prestigious internships from summer to summer, but in those days, many of us still needed to work regular jobs either for reasons of economic necessity or parental insistence. Internships existed in those days of course, but they were far less ubiquitous and regimented than they are today, and most of us—at least in the summers after our freshman and sophomore years—felt no need to get fancy posts in preparation for our future careers in business. We all felt perfectly comfortable waiting tables or tending bar or caddying or doing any number of other pay-by-the-hour jobs when we weren't in class. There was absolutely no shame in it. You didn't feel as if you were falling behind your peers, and there was something oddly liberating about performing tasks where—in contrast to our studies—success was often measured by one's ability to show up on time and do an honest day's work for an honest day's pay, and where, if you were doubly lucky, that pay was also off the books. Summer jobs instilled in me this particular brand of work ethic and, more than that, a basic appreciation for my work and pay. That these things carry over to my generation's work, on Wall Street as in other sectors, seems to me an important thing to bear in mind.

It is almost a cliché for older generations to bemoan the weak work ethic and faulty sense of pride in the waves of youth that follow them. Still, if there is one development I could point to that has contributed mightily to the sense of entitlement and narcissism so apparent in new college graduates from elite universities today, it is the demise of the summer *job*, a position that might require punching a clock, wearing a uniform, and accepting the taunts and orders of those who never went to college and were often proud of it. There are lessons to be learned in finding, getting, and keeping these jobs that don't come from having your father finesse you an internship at Goldman Sachs.

The most important of these lessons, one I learned in the years I spent borrowing my mom's Jeep to deliver papers, driving a campus shuttle bus, or waiting tables in wedding clothes at the Scotto brothers' Fox Hollow Inn, was how lucky I was to be attending college in the first place. Without an education, those jobs might have been a necessary means to pay the bills as opposed to a choice. There is dignity in all work, but it's always better to have options. As a college kid, I greatly enjoyed the fact that my time after work was my own, and the freedom and thrill that came with receiving a paycheck. Today it is not uncommon for me to interview recent college graduates whose work experience consists solely of what one might call the ethereal internship—posts that couldn't be more impressive in terms of status but that also completely inoculate the student from anything remotely resembling real life. I've interviewed kids who spent their summers as "special assistants to the secretary general of the United Nations," or worked in the White House, or roamed the halls of the British Parliament, or spent time—improbably but nobly—helping the poor souls visiting Lourdes.

These are the kinds of wonderful experiences we all wish our kids could enjoy. If these positions present a challenge for those who attain them, it's that they rarely expose the person holding them to unfair treatment, or require them to encounter those whom life has treated poorly. As a result, the holders of such sinecures fail to see that great endeavors often start with learning to complete small, routine tasks; scut work has lessons to teach. Once these tough, thankless summer or part-time jobs ended, I was happy to go back to college, grateful for a chance one shouldn't trifle with. Most of my classmates did the same thing and felt the same way. There were of course traces of the monster that has become the youthful self-esteem cult of today, but such traces were then faint. For the most part, we were happy to be in college and just as happy, with the benefit of time to reflect on them, to have had tedious jobs full of lessons, not the least of which is that many intelligent people, including immigrants and first-generation Americans, had few other options than those jobs we took for granted.

Nevertheless, at a certain point in everyone's life, you realize that your future employers might want some sense that you have a passing interest in the industry of your choice. But three years into school, I still hadn't settled on my industry of choice. In the summer following my junior year at Georgetown in 1989, after spending the first few weeks of summer break at home drinking with my high school buddies and unsuccessfully pursuing the girl who worked behind the counter at Sinatra's pizza on Veterans Highway, I started to piece together something that looked like a résumé, replete with misplaced self-confidence and delusions of grandeur.

For some reason, I was still holding on to the idea that I could use my education in "diplomacy" in the private sector. While it was clear that I wasn't cut out for a career in foreign service or a national security agency, I still had an intense interest in both history and current events. Designed to train diplomats in the aftermath of World War I, the School of Foreign Service at Georgetown has an intense curriculum that requires the completion of courses in political science, history, and economics. A degree from the school also requires proficiency in a foreign language in addition to the university's core curriculum, which included classes in English, theology, and philosophy. Somewhere in this humanities-intensive course load, I discovered that I had a real affinity for macroeconomics. Being able to pair this newfound interest with a real job sounded like a great compromise. Without any real sense of the absurdity of what I was proposing, I listed my career objective as political risk analyst—without really any idea about what such a job might entail—made twenty copies of my résumé on heavy stock paper, and took the Long Island Rail Road into Manhattan to seek my destiny.

I had no set appointments, just a list of companies and their addresses. I walked from Penn Station in my yellow power tie and my ill-fitting suit from Jos. A. Bank, a wonderfully aggressive haberdasher that had held a dress-for-success seminar on campus in the spring semester. I intended to visit the remnants of the great industrial conglomerates of the 1970s; I imagined that Philip Morris, Colgate-Palmolive, ITT, and IBM, among others, might be able to use a guy like me for their far-flung operations. Of course, I never got past the security guard or the receptionist, but I remember that nearly everyone was sympathetic—the way people are with those who seem hopelessly naïve.

My last stop was to visit my cousin Lynn, a loan officer at Republic Bank on Madison Avenue, a welcomingly kind and familiar face after a long day. I went back home and had chicken cutlets and a beer with my dad. I was beat but he seemed proud, perhaps relieved, that I actually had plans to move out of the house upon graduation and to be gainfully employed. He was a kind man who judged people almost solely on their motives and character. A poet, he was a romantic at heart and saw the nobility in those who strive—no matter really what for. I waited for what I hoped would be a series of phone calls from high-powered executives smoking cigars in chalk-striped double-breasted suits who would be certain to yell out to their secretaries something like "Get this kid Trennert on the blower. He might be able to help us with our problems in Johannesburg!" But the calls never came—except for one from a head greenskeeper who needed some extra help at IBM's private country club in Westchester. It is still a wonder to me how my résumé got from Madison and Fifty-seventh to Poughkeepsie, but I was grateful just the same.

My dad urged me to take the job, vaguely referencing what he saw as the start of my own Horatio Alger story in corporate America. I was tempted, too, for I knew the money would be good and the job would put off the reality of coming to terms with my future. But I knew the days of summer jobs with lots of laughs and little responsibility were over. I needed to get something down on paper that demonstrated that I had the "fire in the belly" that so defined the business ethos of the 1980s. So I set my sights a little lower, deleted the pretentious political risk analyst objective from my CV, and set off in my mom's forest-green Cherokee to drop off résumés at the varied brokerage firms that lined Broad Hollow Road in Melville.

There was a lot less security at these firms and it was possible in almost every case to talk to a human being who wasn't so far removed from someone who could hire me, so I felt as if I had a chance. My hit ratio wasn't much better than it had been in Manhattan, but I did receive a call from a broker from Smith Barney: Paul, who needed a cold caller and was willing to give me a chance. Paul was a smart guy who knew what he was doing as best I could tell at the time. He represented much of what most of us strived to be and to have in the rollicking 1980s: in his late twenties, he drove a BMW and was, I later discovered, teaching his gorgeous sales assistant Stephanie to count ceiling tiles in the supply room a few days a week. I was to be paid $200 a week to work Monday through Friday from nine to five, with a fifty-dollar bonus for each new account I opened. I had access to an empty, windowless office, a phone, an enormous Dun and Bradstreet directory of public companies and their top executives, and, finally, to a short script that talked about the "growing opportunities in asset arbitrage" among America's public companies. This was still near the height of the merger boom, and I was expected to make eighty calls a day.

And a strange thing happened, however improbable it sounds to anyone who's worked as a cold caller: I loved it.

I loved the challenge of getting past the secretaries, of pitching new business, of developing some completely apocryphal rap about the market. I loved swapping my Reeboks, khakis, and button-down shirt for a jacket and tie, an ersatz Gordon Gekko in training. Now, looking back at it, the whole idea that I was allowed to call clients unsolicited is shocking to me. But Paul was teaching me the basics and gave me my first copy of *Understanding Wall Street* by Little and Rhodes, still probably the best primer on the stock market available today. In simple terms, it explained the theory of the corporation and the importance of the financial markets in the capital formation process. I developed a new romantic vision of the great industrialists that made America. Few things match the excitement of the young experiencing new endeavors for the first time. I was absolutely thrilled with the idea that I could order my lunch first thing in the morning from a local deli that would deliver it personally to me at lunchtime. I was similarly excited about what would become a staple later on in my life—the after-work watering hole, where brokers and secretaries would imbibe Absolut Citron by the gallon.

There was no voicemail in those days, which in retrospect was a blessing because only the most cynical and experienced secretaries wouldn't take a message if you had the right phone manner and overall demeanor. I can't remember my success rate exactly but my best guess is that perhaps I'd actually be able to talk to three or four "live" prospects for every eighty calls I made, fifty prospect calls being the absolute minimum for a cold caller at the time. One prospect a week might actually take a meeting with Paul. Ultimately, I never received a bonus for actually opening an account, and I was far too stupid to realize that it would be virtually impossible to do so within two months of an introductory phone call. It was a numbers game, pure and simple, and a brutal one at that. What sustained me was learning about the great game of Wall Street and imbibing its lore from both the older brokers and my increasingly expensive desire to read anything I could about the subject.

Wall Street proved a case of love at first sight, perhaps incongruous for me, the son of two public school teachers who had never owned a share of stock in their lives. The pages of my Little and Rhodes book became dog-eared and I wouldn't go out with my friends until nine o'clock on Friday nights for fear of missing Louis Rukeyser's *Wall Street Week*, a precursor—and a better one at that—of the explosion of financial media that would follow it. Physically, he bore some resemblance to George Washington and he possessed the breezy erudition and humor of the quintessential Yankee. It wasn't hard to imagine Lou being the lovable chairman of the board of a company in some black-and-white motion picture. He understood that the little guy could like the stock market, too, and that given the economic circumstances of the 1970s and '80s, many of the topics discussed would naturally straddle both finance and public policy.

The retail brokers assembled at the Smith Barney offices at 445 Broad Hollow Road ran the gamut from serious lifetime agents of their clients' best interests to short-time fraudulent hacks. Back then the process of the media blowing everything completely out of proportion—which would reach its zenith in 1999 during the dot-com era, and again in real estate speculation in the following decade—was in its infancy.

The culture of Wall Street was correspondingly more sober. There were more than a few Vietnam vets in the Broad Hollow office, all serious men at a time when the country was still trying to come to terms with the physical and emotional casualties of America's involvement in that ill-fated war. By far the most unique broker in the office was a Japanese guy named Akio who, through some sort of sick, weird love-hate relationship with his clients, often managed to browbeat them into buying and selling stocks. It wasn't unusual to see him *standing* on his desk, the spiraled telephone cord taut from his excited ministrations, screaming, "You no buy three hundred shares! You buy a thousand shares, dummy!" at the top of his lungs. There are few style points in the brokerage business. Yet somehow it worked—he was a big producer.

As crazy as it might sound, I knew from this suburban Long Island outpost of American finance that Wall Street would be the destination for, and the center of, my professional life. As someone who hungrily devoured public events and was intent on trying to see patterns in varied, unrelated pieces of information, I met my match in Wall Street research, which can be one of the most intellectually stimulating careers one could find. Theoretically, everything—both macro and micro—could yield some investment conclusion or "trade." Wall Street seemed like a practical application—too practical, some of my more public-service-minded friends believed—of what I had hoped to be doing day to day as a foreign service officer or, even more ridiculously, as a spy engaged in espionage, where such research is called "content analysis."

I returned to Georgetown with renewed vigor. For the first time in my life I knew exactly what I wanted to do to earn a living. But I was still an international politics major and so had to cram six economics classes into my senior year. My GPA took a hit, but it was worth it. (Much to my dismay, there was only one correct answer to exam questions in subjects like econometrics as opposed to, let's say, philosophy.) This sense of purpose ultimately made me a better candidate for the jobs for which I would interview.

In those days, everyone at schools like Georgetown wanted to work as an investment banker in general and, in further evidence of the complete cluelessness of people in their early twenties, in particular as M&A specialists. Only later would people realize that in addition to creating financial models, an important function of a two-year analyst position in M&A was to put together pitch books and to reassemble Xerox XJ2000 copiers, which inevitably broke down at two in the morning. Very few people back then thought about going into sales or into trading or, most especially, into the "back office," where I wound up, which is now euphemistically called operations. The banks never bothered to recruit college kids for the research department, perhaps believing we were too stupid to make a real difference in what was seen then, as it is now, a low-margin business. Those jobs were largely reserved for students a few years out of college or possessing an MBA.

For a variety of reasons, not the least of which was the fact that I knew less about finance than probably anyone else interviewing for the same jobs, I received only one offer in investment banking. My interest in the business was too new for me to compete successfully with the kids from Georgetown's business school who studied both theory and the practical application of finance. As luck would have it, the offer came from the ill-fated Drexel Burnham after a Super Saturday in New York, at which you and the other final candidates were flown to New York on a Friday evening, feted and introduced to senior management, and then spent an entire day at the firm's headquarters interviewing for the final spots on Saturday. I learned I received an offer the next morning by telephone. For the son of two English teachers from a small town where there were no investment bankers, this was heady stuff. Unfortunately, the first rung on my corporate ladder gave way rather suddenly. Two days later the company would close its doors for good. Welcome to Wall Street, pal.

No doubt the people who gave me the offer were just as blind-sided by the bank's closing as I was, but this episode with Drexel was my first introduction to the concept that few people were going to look out for my best interests better than I would. It also was an object lesson in the idea that despite the reputation for bravado and the celebration of the swashbuckler, Wall Street wasn't a particularly good place to make enemies.

By the late 1980s, Drexel Burnham Lambert was the fifth-largest investment bank in the United States and becoming synonymous with the use of junk bonds (now known as high-yield bonds) to finance start-ups and companies that had fallen on hard times. Later on, the firm's "highly confident" letter assured financiers that it could use those bonds to finance the increasingly popular practice of hostile takeovers. The leader of this revolution was Drexel's very own Michael Milken. He was the first to discover the relatively low default rates of the bonds of "fallen angels," an interesting and important development in finance. Unfortunately, like a lot of human endeavors in which obscene amounts of money can be made, the practice of issuing junk bonds got out of hand, ultimately resulting in unethical and illegal activity that led to the firm's downfall. Foreshadowing in some small way what happened to Bear Stearns a little less than twenty years later, there had been a small chance in February 1990 that loan guarantees from the U.S. government could have saved Drexel.

I only learned of this many years later. Tragically, the Fates had insisted on exacting some sort of poetic justice on the firm, and on a cosmic scale. A pioneer in the practice of leveraged buyouts, Drexel had engineered one of its first hostile takeovers in 1985; the target company was Unocal. At the time, Unocal's investment banker was Dillon Read, whose former chairman, Nicholas Brady, later became secretary of the treasury and, ultimately, the arbiter of Drexel's fate. Brady had never forgiven Drexel for its role in the hostile bid for Unocal and wouldn't even consider putting taxpayers' money at risk to save a firm he detested. A little less than two decades later, Bear's failure could be traced in part to its refusal to participate in the bailout of Long-Term Capital Management. The Wall Street banks tasked with making the hedge fund's many counterparties whole after its collapse in 1998 had similarly never forgiven Bear Stearns for its refusal to take part in the bailout. When the music stopped for Bear in March 2008, it had few friends among its competitors. The wheels of justice on Wall Street sometimes turn slowly, almost painfully so, but they turn just the same.

In the end, I was able to secure a job—a bad one by the standards of my classmates—at a storied "white-shoe" investment firm with a great reputation for propriety, Morgan Stanley. I was to rotate among the firm's many operations areas, looking for a spot where I might be able to help out permanently. This would mean a year spent as a glorified gofer. I started out in the New Accounts department, securing and then inputting client information into the company's computers, before spending time on the floor of the New York Stock Exchange as a clerk; next, I helped clear equity trades in a department called Purchase and Sales before putting in time in the appropriately named "cage," where I clipped bond coupons from physical securities and mailed out statements. Most of these jobs have been automated by now, and if they exist at all are likely to be completed in cities with considerably less expensive office space than New York.

I learned quickly that my job in the back office put me about as far away from the intellectual challenge of making investment decisions as I could get. An interest in current affairs and public economic policy was about as useful in that job as the ability to play the violin. The operations side of the business rarely interacted with the firm's clients—certainly never in person—and was concerned solely with the critical assembly-line clerical work of clearing billions of dollars in trades every day. Those who populated these back office roles ranged from the kind and the striving to the irreplaceably broken and hostile. In his book *The Go-Go Years*, about the markets in the late 1960s, famed Wall Street scribe John Brooks tried to explain the phenomenon of people who would trade the best years of their lives in the back office for the chance to get lucky:

> Why, then, did they come at all? For a dream of glamour; for the chance to handle or merely to be close to great sums of money; for the chance to be "where the action was"; or simply out of curiosity and the quest for experience, to find out "what Wall Street is like." Or, indeed, even for prestige: to be able to say, in the local bar or the social club, "Don't tell me about Wall Street. I work there," and to watch the heads turn and the eyes widen and be asked for a hot tip on the market. What did they ask for? A living, a sense of doing a

job, office companionship, the possibility of meeting a date or a mate—the things youth asks of routine office jobs everywhere. An ambitious few dreamed the old Wall Street dream of rising from clerk to partner. But what most of them found was tedium, disappointment, long hours, quasimilitary discipline, occasional racial flare-ups, and finally, the nightmarish frustration of being called upon to do what simply could not be done in good order and in good time.*

At the time, it wasn't uncommon for even many of the institutional salesmen and traders of the front office to lack "book learnin'." In the back office it was considered even less necessary to have a formal education. This didn't bother me as much as the fact that a college degree was often seen as a threat and a liability to those I worked for. "College boy" was commonly thrown my way contemptuously with every one of my frequent mistakes.

To use an industrial comparison, I desperately wanted to be in the design or sales department but was stuck on the factory floor. What made matters worse is that Morgan's back office was in Brooklyn—a galaxy away it seemed from my pinstriped heroes at Morgan Stanley's headquarters at 1251 Avenue of the Americas. For a time, I was seated next to an old guy who spent his daily lunch hour collecting aluminum cans to cash in the deposit. I took this as a bad sign. It became clear pretty quickly that not only was I not on the corporate ladder but also that the ladder was likely to remain hidden from me. I didn't help my cause by insisting on dressing like a complete Wall Street tool, a poor man's Gordon Gekko surrounded by a sea of functionaries clad in threadbare

---

* John Brooks, *The Go-Go Years*, New York: John Wiley and Sons, Inc., 1973, 1998, 196.

polyester suits and flame-retardant dress shirts. Let's just say that I wasn't exactly a heartbeat away from the corner office.

Seventeen years later, during the financial crisis of 2008—as the media increasingly focused on toppling figures of power and wealth on Wall Street—I thought a lot about this phase of my career. For certain, Wall Street has had far more than its fair share of ultrawealthy jerks, but it also employs many more thousands of people who take the subway to work and worry about paying their mortgage every month. My colleague who collected cans "worked on Wall Street" in a sense, but he was part of this industry's invisible and low-paid human machinery, and he isn't what the press had in mind when it started talking about exacting some "retribution" from New York City's principal industry.

During this Brooklyn sojourn, my psychological state was greatly compromised by the end of my first real love affair. It was, of course, with "the blonde," a young woman reminiscent of Angie Dickinson in her prime. An Italian American with a penchant for old movies, I thought of myself as a poor man's Dean Martin, and my relationship with her slowly took on the character of a cross between *Who's Afraid of Virginia Woolf?* and the *amour fou* of Frank Sinatra and Ava Gardner.

I was certainly in love with this woman, but I now wonder whether I was more in love with the vanity associated with my relationship with her. It was—and still is to a certain extent—incomprehensible to me that any great beauty could be in love with me. I was too insecure to believe that a beautiful WASP would be attracted to some tawny Wop from Long Island. Without an Iago to provoke me, I learned of the great inner torture of jealousy. Our affair ended as all such matters of the heart must: tragically and badly, my self-doubt and jealousy dooming the relationship practically from the beginning.

Unfortunately, I was too young at that point to realize that this was no great tragedy; it was simply one of life's disappointments and a banal one at that. It was a rite of passage that I mistook for the last rites. I magnified the consequences of the breakup as much as I did the relationship itself and entered a period of sadness, darkness, and shame about my behavior—often involving ridiculous bouts of potvaliancy—that I found hard to shake for almost a year.

Heaven sent me salvation in the form of two buddies from Georgetown, John Crager and Jay Coyle. Crager was an accounting major, whose quiet nature belied an offbeat sense of humor. Coyle was a finance major and, like me, worked at Morgan Stanley in a department called Streamline, in which it seemed his primary function was to figure which departments could get away with having one secretary instead of two. We created our own fraternity house of sorts on Eighty-second Street, a walk-up with a backyard that was perfect for what would be a series of parties over the next two years, parties that would rival the best times I ever had in college, replete with keg stands, chick props ("Here's a picture of me and Sammy Hagar—we're buddies"), absurd mating rituals, and lots of laughs. It was also in that backyard, I should add, that I would eventually encounter another one of the Lord's tender mercies toward me—my future wife, Bevin.

Before that celestial development, even by the standards of a refugee camp or a cruise ship adrift in the Gulf of Mexico, our three-bedroom duplex was revolting and eerily reminiscent of Delta House. It was so bad that one day after work I spent an entire hour in the apartment before I realized it had been ransacked and the few valuables we owned stolen. Most of the girls we dated preferred to use the bathroom across the street at Brady's, a bar that catered to rumpots whose average age was around eighty. The highlight of our two years there was coming home at two in the morning after one of our parties to find a man's shirt, pants, and shoes *nailed* to the wall in our living room. This act summed up some of the best years of our lives.

There comes a time when all of that stuff gets old, particularly when your career isn't progressing as quickly as you'd like. After about a year, the laughs remained at the bars in the evening with my buddies. The despair on the subway to work only grew, especially when I passed Bowling Green, the last subway stop on the 4 train from Manhattan. Despite the good times and the excitement of at least being able to say that I worked for the great investment bank Morgan Stanley, an anxious emptiness remained. My career wasn't close to being what I wanted it to be, and my confidence was shot. Before I met Bevin, on my way to work I would sometimes duck into St. Ignatius on Eighty-fourth and Park to beg—"outlaw-wise"—for some sort of reconciliation with my old girlfriend as well as for the professional life I thought I deserved, my forehead and index finger moist as I walked back out into the humid dawns of Manhattan. Desperate to make my way in the world of my chosen profession, I knew that I had miles to go before I could sleep. I didn't realize yet that luck, fickle and unstable, could sometimes turn good.

2

A LITTLE LUCK

If there was one thing that tempered my worries about getting stuck in the back office, it was that Morgan Stanley in those days offered a number of classes on the business at its headquarters. If you were willing, there were any number of classes you could take after hours on a variety of financial topics at 1251 Avenue of the Americas. Not particularly accustomed to working or getting up early, I was prone, like my friend Jay, to being out cold during these classes, but still they were there if you wanted to avail yourself of them. I was also given the chance to take my Series 7, the fabled test to become a "registered representative," more popularly known as a stockbroker. Then, as now, the test was six hours long and required serious preparation. The concepts weren't particularly hard but the amount of material was significant.

Putting into practice Bud Fox's line to Gordon Gekko in *Wall Street,* "Life comes down to a few moments . . . this is one of them," I took the test more seriously than I needed to, believing that this single exam held the key to my future. The company graciously paid for prep classes I took at Loews Summit Hotel on Lexington Avenue and Fifty-first in Midtown. My classmates were a strange mix of college kids, boiler room guys, and sales assistants, most of whom were pretty young women. The teacher, a short stocky guy with a smile that made him look like a character from a Dr. Seuss book, appeared to me to be a grizzled veteran, but he was probably no older than twenty-eight. He was a very successful interest rate trader for a large investment bank. This was a big deal and most assuredly meant that he was making well into the six figures. After we became friends, I asked him why he would waste his time teaching rookies municipal securities rules and options strategies. He looked at me as if I were the dumbest guy on God's green earth. "It's easier to get laid teaching a Series Seven class than at the Limelight," he said simply, referring to a popular nightclub of the time. For a lot of men, it never changes; it's always all about women.

When I wasn't in the middle of almost heroic drinking sessions with my buddies, I studied for the exam very seriously, taking the practice tests so often that I practically had them memorized. By the spring of 1991, I was ready to sit the test, scheduled for a sunny April Thursday in a drab office building on Broad Street. In what has become a hallmark of my life—to exaggerate the importance of just about everything—I got up at 6:00 a.m. and took a run around the reservoir in Central Park, the first and last time I ever did that, incidentally. Then I took the East Side subway to Fulton Street and had a cup of coffee and a doughnut in the shadow of George Washington on the steps of the Federal Building. I gazed up at the frieze that adorned the New York Stock Exchange—INTEGRITY PROTECTING THE WORKS OF MAN—and saw this as a transformative moment on my journey from Long Island punk to Manhattan guru.

One of the first to take the exam by computer, I learned that I had passed the test on the spot. Thrilled, I proceeded directly to a bar called Suspenders at 111 Broadway and ran into some Morgan Stanley folks, including one of the principal managers of its back office, a guy I'll call Sal Mustachio. Full of myself and well into my cups, I regaled my older comrades and some of the girls with tales of my projected future success, postulating about the "deals" I was likely to engineer. That I had no money and was hopelessly in debt did not deter me from using my credit card to buy rounds for my new friends. I was on. I was funny. And I was well on my way. I remember going home with a girl named Patty, who my friends later affectionately referred to as Panty for reasons that need not be elaborated here. I woke up the next day and actually made it to work on time. Two hours later, I got a call from Sal's secretary.

"Mr. Mustachio would like you to come up to his office at eleven."

"Sure thing," I replied.

After what seemed like an eternity laboring in complete anonymity (but was, in reality, ten months), my high self-regard was bruised, and I perceived my considerable talents to be wasted. But with my new Series 7 license, I was now likely to be promoted— or even brought up to "the show" in Manhattan. You can't keep a good man down. It was my time.

At the appointed hour, I arrived at Sal's office.

"Take a seat," he said gruffly. He wasn't quite the jovial guy I remembered from the night before.

"Sure, what's up, Sal?"

"First of all it's Mr. Mustachio. I have socks older than you."

"Um . . . yeah sure, Mr. Mustachio." I immediately realized I had made a slight miscalculation here; this would not be a victory lap.

"Are you sure this industry is for you?"

I was stunned, and after a pause I stammered, "But I love Wall Street. This is what I want to do."

"No, you love the *idea* of Wall Street. The back office is no place for dreamers in yellow suspenders, kid."

"I thought I might be able to work my way up."

"No one works their way up from down here to go up there. You oughta settle in for the grind or find another place to work."

After another two minutes protesting my genuine affection for the business and the firm, I was told to go back to work and keep a lower profile. Given the fact that my main competition at the Brooklyn office was the rummy who collected aluminum cans on his lunch hour, this was a rather inauspicious development in my career plans.

Predictably, I was depressed. Only later did I learn that Sal was wrong. It was difficult to get from the back office to the front office, but it wasn't impossible. At the time, I figured I was doomed to a life of processing trades in Brooklyn Heights. And while the executive suite at Morgan still sported oil paintings of WASPs and the firm's general counsel wore a bowler hat at the time, Wall Street was indeed changing. It was still relatively rare, but kids from the boroughs or who weren't in any way to the manor born were making their way into the upper echelons of finance through grit, smarts, and hard work. Georgetown was a great school, but it merely got you the opportunity to get a spot at the firm. After that, no one cared about your desire for self-actualization; you were there simply, as it should be, to serve the interests of the firm's shareholders. But I was impatient and, more important, I was stupid. I thought Mustachio was right and that my future at the firm was doomed.

I'd heard the name John Mack, then head of the Fixed Income department on his way to chairing the firm's operating committee, but I just assumed he was another blueblood in charge. Only later did I learn that he was the product of Lebanese immigrants who ran a small supermarket in North Carolina. His shadow didn't darken the Gothic arches of Yale or the Georgian halls of Harvard but rather the granite arches and spires of Duke, a school located in his native state that he attended on a football scholarship. In my year at the firm, I never saw the man. People referred to him as Darth Vader, like some mythic figure, but he was almost invisible to employees at my level. This was just as well. He was known to be tough—someone you didn't want to tangle with.

I did have the occasion to run into another up-and-comer: John Havens, the head of equity sales and trading, who appeared all the more menacing because he appeared to be completely hairless. Vague rumors swirled around the firm about how he got that way. The most fantastic version of the story was that he was bitten, in comic book–like fashion, by a rare insect in Africa while on safari. As a result he lost all his hair but was compensated, it was assumed, by receiving the gift of almost superhuman powers of toughness and, more important, of having shed any remnant of his conscience.

One of the things they never tell you in a college career office is that getting the job just means that you get a chance to play in the game. If you're lucky the game will be fair and hard work will be rewarded, but no such guarantee exists. And the concept of a true mentor for a rookie, at least on Wall Street, is so absurd that if anyone actually told me such a person existed today I would consider him the perpetrator of some cruel practical joke. No one really promises you such a person during the recruiting process, but it's often implied that some mandarin will guide your career from the beginning. The reality is that no one—absolutely no one—except you can sustainably be relied on to care about your career at a large company.

And so in the spring of 1991 I was penniless, forlorn, and had just been told by Sal that my future at a major Wall Street firm was tenuous. But I did have my Series 7 and that should count for something, shouldn't it? Not knowing what else to do, I went to the Yellow Pages. My copy was currently acting as a TV stand, so, after removing the snowy-screened, rabbit-eared box from its pedestal, I searched for the phone numbers of employment agencies and executive research firms. I wrote down the names of five companies on a white index card, fashioned another résumé, and mailed it out. The first and only call I got back was from a company called Smyth and Associates that was representing a start-up research boutique headed by a legendary economist by the name of Ed Hyman. At the time, *Institutional Investor* had ranked Ed the number one economist on Wall Street, ten years in a row. I had never heard of the man but the job sounded as if it might get me a little closer to what I loved about the business.

Preparing for an interview in those days was a little more difficult than it would be today: there were no quick Internet searches. One evening after work, I visited Morgan's extensive library in Midtown. Using the microfiche machine, I researched my new potential boss and made copies at ten cents a pop of his interviews with *Barron's* and of his profiles in *Fortune*. What emerged from these profiles was a man of good humor who clearly loved talking about the economy and the financial markets. A week later, I arrived at his new firm's offices at 717 Fifth Avenue and was greeted by a woman who was about six feet tall if she was an inch. I followed her into Ed's office.

Shortly after, a man no taller than five-three walked into the room, followed by a woman several inches shorter (in heels). This was Ed, and his partner, Nancy Lazar. I started to wonder whether a bearded lady or a guy on stilts would be part of the interview process. Ed was warm and exuded the breezy charm of his native West Texas; the somewhat lockjawed Nancy was circumspect. Ed started in immediately, focusing on the one item on my résumé that had never drawn as much as an aside in the dozens of interviews I had with investment banks while I was in college or, for that matter, when I actually had a job at one.

"How did you like cold calling?" he asked simply.

"Actually, I liked it. It was a challenge."

"In what way?" he pressed.

"Well, mainly, because no one really wants to talk to you. So the trick is to try to pick up on something that would give you the slightest chance of keeping them on the phone."

"How do you do that?"

"I don't know. Maybe it's the accent. Perhaps it's the mood they're in. It was hard but if you could get to thirty seconds you actually had a shot at an appointment for a follow-up phone call. You make eighty phone calls a day for a few months and you got to be a pretty good judge of people. Time was your friend."

Ed smiled, perhaps realizing he had found someone just innocent enough to take a chance on a start-up. He asked me to come back a week later and offered me a job as an institutional salesman. After a halfhearted attempt to negotiate a higher salary, I accepted the job. Ed had quickly picked up on the fact that I was desperate, cheap, and willing to work hard.

I resigned from Morgan Stanley and gave them my two weeks' notice. I was nervous and thought I would be subjected to some mistreatment for my treachery. Unsurprisingly, no attempt was made to keep me. My last day was July 3, 1991, my tenure at Morgan ending at precisely one year. On my last day I ran into Sal, or rather Mr. Mustachio, in the cafeteria at Morgan's Brooklyn Heights office.

"So I hear you're leaving?"

I nodded. "Yeah, we'll see. It's a start-up."

"You're leaving Morgan Stanley to go to a start-up?" he asked, shaking his head in disgust.

It was like dealing with Joe Pesci's character in *Goodfellas*: "Funny how, like a clown? Do I amuuuuse you?" You'd never win with Sal; it was time for a change. But still, the idea of leaving a firm like Morgan Stanley for a start-up was not nearly as common then as it might be now. At the time, it was seen as a little like voluntarily transferring from Harvard to Suffolk County Community College.

I had one day off before I was to start my new job and on July 4, 1991, I watched the Yankees beat the Orioles 3–2 from the bleachers under the hot summer sun at the stadium. I drank cold beer and, between screaming vulgarities at Orioles outfielder David Segui in right, I pondered my job at a start-up company called International Strategy and Investment, to begin the next day. A year out of Georgetown, my major accomplishments on Wall Street were passing the Series 7 and getting the pizza order right for the traders at Morgan Stanley. It was a beautiful summer day on which I felt, alone watching a game I loved in a city I couldn't do without, something bordering on contentment.

I started work on a Friday. As I remember it, I was the eleventh employee hired at a company that was only three months old. Nancy introduced me around and escorted me to the room that was to house the firm's only four institutional salesmen. I knew I was home when we started our morning meeting by discussing the day's research. There was a lot of talk of the federal taxes and spending, the Federal Reserve system, inflation, the relative attractiveness of bonds to stocks, and how the markets closed in Japan. In short, it was everything I thought I would be discussing when I graduated from college. For the first time my chosen field of study seemed relevant and it was a relief. But while mention of research made a welcome change, many of the words thrown around during the meeting were Greek to me. My diary from that time reveals how utterly bewildered I was by the concepts discussed. I scrawled in big block letters across the first page of my first notebook: REVIEW RELATIONSHIP BETWEEN BONDS AND INFLATION.

I was convinced I would be revealed as a fraud and fined every day for the next six months.

In addition to the fact that there was a morning research meeting in which it was considered a plus to have read the newspaper and to have at least a passing familiarity with what was going on in the financial markets, this was also the first time in my life that I started to be aware of others' wealth and to observe firsthand those who had developed expensive tastes. People had enough money to buy clothes that actually fit and they were able, with a straight face, to make value judgments about the quality of wine or the talents of the bartender mixing them a martini. This is important for the would-be Wall Streeter because, as Damon Runyon once advised, "Always try to rub up against money, for if you rub up against money long enough, some of it might rub off on you."

Ed Hyman was so popular that he had been sent dozens of bottles of champagne upon the start of his new firm. In an act of magnanimity that was a vestige of the Wall Street partnerships from bygone days, he decided to share his bounty with the firm every Friday at 4:00 p.m. after the market closed, and he kept the tradition going long after the original bottles ran dry. That small act of kindness still amazes me and we have instituted the same practice at my firm today. The only slight difference is that we serve beer and wine—haven't graduated to the champagne stage yet.

At the close of that first day at ISI, standing around a conference table from which the champagne was flowing, I was feeling, for a moment, good about my new gig. Then I met a bond salesman who would later become one of my best friends in the business, an Irishman from New Jersey named Patrick Alwell. The first of seven kids, he was the older ballbuster brother I never had and remains one of the greatest living examples of Freud's alleged observation that the Irish were "one race of people for whom psychoanalysis is of no use whatsoever." Pat sidled up to me and asked, "You ever hear of a thing called sunscreen?"

My new colleagues laughed. I was so tan from my day at the Yankee game that it looked like I had either never worked a day in my life or had just arrived on a steamer from Palermo. I was somewhat embarrassed and my ears, the only part of my face that could register the emotion, flushed.

"Hi, I'm Jason Trennert, but my friends call me Jase," I said, trying to charm my way out of a confrontation with a guy who enjoyed breaking other people's balls.

"You excited about your new career on Wall Street, *Jase*?"

"Yeah, this is a great opportunity. I love Wall Street."

"Oh really," he said. "Let me show you something." Then he drew a graph on a piece of paper that looked like this:

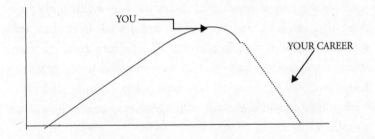

"You see this big point here?" he asked.

"Yeah."

"Well," he said triumphantly. "This is you. See this dotted line here?"

"Yeah."

"Well, this is where our industry and your career are going."

At that point he threw the paper up in the air, dramatically underscoring the hopelessness of my situation. Scarcely nine hours into my chance at fame and fortune as a Wall Street financier, a nattily dressed, glib Irishman with a pocket square told me that my career was essentially over before it had started. Having attended Georgetown and having a propensity to drink and see the ironies of life, I had run into my fair share of guys like Pat. Through the years, I have found many of my best friends to be Irish. None of them are even remotely as sensitive as my Italian friends, for whom imperceptible slights can take decades to work themselves out, and who, while they might be able to bench-press three hundred pounds, might cry if their mother yells at them. Perhaps as a result of the number of kids in the family and the often *Lord of the Flies* nature of the homes they grew up in, the Irish were a little different. There was no ambiguity when they wanted to offend you or make you laugh. And so it was with Pat.

I was a little hurt and embarrassed but I had learned not to let on for fear that the ribbing would only get worse. Privately, I took his warning seriously and somewhat personally. Only years later, after he had become one of my best friends in the business, would I realize that Pat was one of Wall Street's great salesmen, showmen, and bullshit artists. He, maybe more than any other colleague on Wall Street, taught me to develop a healthy distrust of both good and bad news, and of drawing easy conclusions about people.

I shared an office with three other institutional equity salesmen and we all eventually became good friends. On my first day, two of them, Frank and Alan, greeted me with a long debate, conducted as if I weren't in the room, about whether my glasses were too big for my face (they were). Stephanie, my third officemate, was a short, pretty blonde whose understanding of the industry far exceeded her two decades on the planet. Sensing that an attractive girl could turn three otherwise level-headed guys in their twenties into complete morons, she sometimes pitted us against each other to get what she wanted—from desirable vacation days to preferred use of the fax machine—in yet another indication that we were amateurs in the great game of finance.

We were all part of something new and exciting and the company was almost immediately successful, which helped. The four of us were given the unusual and fortuitous opportunity to split the entire universe of institutional investors in the United States among ourselves. In addition to the New York accounts we all shared, I was given Boston and the Southeast as my territories and it marked the first time in my life I was handed responsibility for something that could affect the livelihoods of others. I felt grateful, proud, and, for the first time once again, a little bit like an adult.

We were well paid and while much was expected of us, we were very well treated. My new colleagues and I spent a lot of our off time together doing what most people in their twenties did then and what, for the most part, my colleagues and I still do today, the only real difference being that we didn't have to check in with anyone back then. And if we did, we would have had to find a pay phone in one of the bars on the Upper East Side to explain why we were once again late, had had too much to drink, and had not yet eaten dinner.

Long before it became fashionable in Silicon Valley or in other businesses with absurdly high margins or an absurdly low cost of capital, Wall Street adopted the concept of open architecture on its trading floors. This wasn't a part of some hippy-dippy management theory or any sense among Wall Street's buttoned-up partnerships of the need to "bond." Open trading floors without much privacy were simply a function of the fact that information on securities prices was scarce, expensive, and opaque. This meant that you had to be able to see and hear the person with whom you were transacting business. Today, you could trade bonds with another member of your firm sitting ten feet away from you without uttering a word. In the old days, you might have a phone in each hand while simultaneously trying to relay information to a colleague. It might be hard to believe but it is a relatively new phenomenon that much of the business was even conducted indoors. The American Stock Exchange, commonly known as the curb, transacted all of its business outdoors on Broad Street until 1921, its brokers on telephones straining to signal their colleagues on the street from the open windows of the offices above.

Of course, the Amex doesn't exist anymore, having merged with the New York Stock Exchange in 2008. Ticker tape machines were commonly in use until the 1960s and it wasn't uncommon for a junior trader on an equity desk to get his fills for stock orders ten minutes after a trade was transacted, a single ticker tape having passed through the hands of as many as twenty-five traders before the price could be confirmed. Today, pricing information for stocks can be found from any number of sources for free, but with a delay of fifteen minutes, or the prices can be had in real time for anyone with modest sums to trade online.

One of the open secrets of trading desks is that they are inordinately fun places to work for those with hopeless cases of arrested development who long for the days of high school locker-room wisecracks and towel snapping. The industry's rules of engagement in terms of language, sexual innuendo, and skirt chasing, while largely diminished elsewhere, remain on the trading floor among the most robust in our now politically correct world. Although tame by last generation's standards, the Wall Street trading floor remains one of the most masculine—and fun—places to work in all of corporate life.

Not everyone enjoys it, of course. The Wall Street professional unable to laugh at himself or to cope with a complete lack of privacy should seek work in corporate finance or in human resources or in some other department of a company—one that features office walls. I didn't grow up with brothers or sisters and, though I played baseball through high school and college, I had never been teased as mercilessly as I was when I first started my career on Wall Street. Within my first week, it was clear that many of my more hard-boiled and wizened colleagues used insults as masterfully as Michelangelo used a paintbrush. Unless you grew up as the youngest son of a large Irish family, there was little to prepare you for the verbal assaults that awaited you. This is yet more difficult when you're young and when the rules of engagement concerning your responses are unclear. You have to fight back enough to be left alone but not so much that you offend someone who could really make your life miserable. It becomes more fun when your ego grows callused and you can start to fight back.

Sitting cheek by jowl with other educated and competitive people quickly creates a culture that regulates the way one dresses, acts, and speaks. What is often most shocking for my friends outside the industry who have spent any time with me on the trading floor is the familiarity with which senior and junior people can interact and also the sheer amount of wagering that goes on among the salesmen and traders when they aren't on the phone with clients. A little bit like Sky Masterson from a Damon Runyon short story, guys will bet on anything from the speed at which two raindrops will fall to the bottom of a windowsill to the gender, weight, and sometimes even the race of a co-worker's newborn.

The funny thing about a lot of traders, at least those who last, is just how risk averse they are when it comes to wagering large amounts of their own money in financial assets, the subject one would presume they know best. The same guy who didn't mind betting and losing a grand on some midseason Big East game is also likely to have 80 percent of his personal fortune in money market funds and Treasury securities. In the years between the market bottom in 1982 and the financial crisis in 2008, I found that it was often the senior executives long since removed from the trading culture that tended to take the biggest chances with their personal wealth. This had a lot to do, in my view, with what economists call moral hazard. Without putting too fine a point on it, investors were well served to buy financial assets after every correction. This feeling became so ingrained that many thought they couldn't lose. The most senior executives had simply seen this phenomenon play out for a longer period of time, had the most to lose, and consequently got themselves into the most trouble financially.

There are downsides to life on a trading desk, of course: the long hours, the noise, the complete lack of privacy, and the intense pressure to produce can lead to bad habits after the day has ended. It's a business that prides itself, perhaps more than any other, on the free flow of information. Being well read and well informed is essential. For the news junkie, it can be among the more intellectually stimulating businesses one can find. Following every bit of news to hit the tape every day from 8:00 a.m. to 4:00 p.m. can, over time, make it difficult to think strategically. If there is a benefit, it is a healthy respect for risk and a deeply ingrained habit to look at all decisions in both your professional and personal life in risk-versus-reward terms.

At this point you're probably wondering how guys that I claim are so good at risk management have come so close in recent years to completely blowing up the entire financial system. The answer is simple: Wall Street traders had been increasingly incentivized to take risks not with their own money, not with the money of partners who might sit ten feet away from them, but with the money of thousands of faceless and long-distance shareholders of a public company. Losses might result in a smaller bonus or dismissal that was easily forgotten in the heady days of a bubble, but big enough trading profits over a relatively short period of time can set up a trader and his bosses financially for life. The death of the Wall Street partnership has been one of the single biggest—and perhaps most deleterious—changes on Wall Street. Greater systemic risk and the "too big to fail" phenomenon have been the result.

My favorite part of those early days at ISI, and a daily ritual that has been part of my professional life for the past twenty-five years, was those morning research meetings. At the time we all thought it started relatively early—8:00 a.m.—an hour and a half before the market opened for trading. That start time seems laughably late now when many Wall Street firms start their morning research meetings at 7:00 a.m. to "keep the casino open" as long as possible. What was even better about these meetings than being spoon-fed research to communicate to our clients was that the best salesmen, like Pat, were extraordinarily well read and up-to-date on market-moving news, on economic events, and on all the counterarguments. In the social sciences, there really are no controlled experiments; there are simply too many moving pieces. Understanding where the consensus thought securities prices were going allows the talented investor opportunities to bet against it. Reading *The Wall Street Journal* and *Barron's* were seen as the bare minimum, and Ed and Nancy read through no less than nine newspapers every day in preparation for the day's research. Their day started at 6:30 a.m. to get a report ready for the 8:00 a.m. research meeting. The level of dedication and commitment to succeed was unlike anything I had ever seen. It was clear that their success was by no means an accident and that we were expected to show the same level of dedication to the business in spirit if not in action.

In those early days at ISI I was often struck by just how large a role luck, both good and bad, could play in one's career. By any objective standard, I should never have been given that ISI job. I remain in awe of and forever grateful for the chance my new bosses gave me.

3

PLAYERS TRAVEL LIGHT

Only a man who spends a considerable part of his life on an airplane can know just how beautiful the Bulova Building in Queens can be at five in the morning. Its art deco design conveys such a sense of power and wealth that one could assume Ayn Rand herself had designed it.

If you work on Wall Street as an institutional salesman, investment banker, or securities analyst, you know the building all too well. Near LaGuardia Airport, it is one of the few recognizable landmarks in what can be a dreary ride from the Upper East Side through postindustrial America over the RFK Triborough Bridge and on your way to the airport. At dawn, it signifies both the relief of having escaped the city with a reasonably good chance at making your flight and the dread of knowing that you are about to deal with the assorted charmers that comprise the commercial airline industry in the United States. In the dead and tense cold of an early winter morning, the sight of the building still moves me, usually still half-asleep, to deep existential questions. Does the Bulova watch company still exist? How many people worked there? How did they afford such a beautiful edifice? Is

God really everywhere? Why doesn't everyone choose to live someplace warm? Who invented liquid soap and why?

Of all the modern "conveniences" hailed in the postwar years as a boon to both the workingman and housewife alike—the affordable automobile, television, air-conditioning, white goods, and pharmaceuticals for any conceivable ailment real or imagined—it might be safe to say that they have all improved in terms of reliability and ease of use. One of the great ironies of the modern era is that the quality of manufactured goods has improved dramatically at the same time the quality of customer service has declined. One would think this would be impossible in the U.S. economy, 85 percent of which is comprised of services, only 15 percent manufacturing. The vanguard of the "we can treat you however we like and you've got to take it" movement in many service-oriented industries is the commercial airline business. If there is a more depressing and dehumanizing form of human transportation for the average guy in the gray flannel suit, I have yet to find it.

My best friend growing up on Long Island, Marcus, was the product of German immigrants: a flight attendant mother and a father who was a purser for Pan American Airways in the golden age of air travel. They would often charm us with stories of their encounters with Audrey Hepburn or Mario Andretti or Henry Kissinger and it all seemed so glamorous. It didn't hurt that she looked like Elke Summer and he had the easy demeanor and good humor of one of those elegant European actors from black-and-white motion pictures. Of course, only the rich could really afford to fly in those days, before the airplane had become a bus with wings or, as comedian Dennis Miller once put it, a "bad restaurant at thirty thousand feet."

The whole process of flying has become so unpleasant that one can't help but think that Warren Buffett was right when he said

that as far as investors were concerned, it would have saved everyone a lot of time and money if Orville and Wilbur Wright were
shot out of the sky on their first attempt. Of course the seeds of
the destruction of the customer experience were sown with the
deregulation of the industry in the 1970s, which opened flight
routes to competition and, tragically, to the events of 9/11. The
first development allowed any yahoo in shorts to travel from Bay
City to Portland in February for sixty-nine bucks; the second introduced a newly dysfunctional government bureaucracy into our
lives that is putatively charged with passenger safety. Near-constant
business travel has led me to come to the conclusion that the TSA's
chances of actually catching a bad guy are only slightly higher than
me randomly passing a sailboat during my next morning consti-
tutional.

The airline industry has disappointed and inconvenienced
me in ways so varied that my only choice has been to develop a
Zen-like attitude toward the whole process. I have been subjected
to canceled flights and long delays for reasons ranging from
thunderstorm-related ground stops at Kennedy to a Central American woman's attempts to put her chinchilla through an X-ray
machine to a poor kid's anxiety attack during his first international
flight. To make matters worse, all of this, plus the poor economics of the industry, has turned the attractive and upbeat flight at-
tendants of years past into often insufferably bitter sky waitresses
without even the slightest trace of the milk of human kindness.
The real players in the investment business fly private of course,
but after twenty-five years I have only experienced that joy twice—
both times on a client's dime. Flying first class is no longer a given
on today's Wall Street and is largely only granted if the flight is
long enough (four hours or more) to make it impossible to be productive upon landing.

The fair-minded must admit that many of the modern indig-

nities are not entirely the fault of the airlines themselves. Weather
and safety concerns have turned what was once actually fun and
predictable into a stressful game in which there is no consistency
for the frequent business traveler. One week at Bay City International you have to check in thirty minutes prior to departure. The
next week in Timbuktu, it's forty-five minutes, and oh, by the way,
your carry-on has to be gate checked. If you live your life on the
road working as a sell-side analyst or institutional salesman, you
might visit a number of different cities and take a variety of flights
in a single week, all the while attempting to balance work and
family responsibilities at home. Such varied procedures put you
in a constant and exhausting state of stress. Having to watch *Hope
Floats* or any of the other painfully saccharine and stupid romantic comedies the airlines serve up as entertainment does little to
ease the tension. It is little wonder then that a recent study of
wealthy families by *Barron's* concluded that engaging the services
of a private jet company is often the *first* decision those who have
attained a certain net worth will make.

But for the middle-class-kid-cum-finance-professional-with-
an-expense-account, there were few things more exciting than the
prospect of business travel, especially abroad. In those early years
at ISI, dreams of chance encounters with captains of industry and
mysterious women occurred frequently. On the occasion of my
first trip to Atlanta in 1991, I was so excited that I was actually
getting paid to travel I brought a camera, a sandwich, my Walk-
man with several tapes of hair bands from the eighties, and a book
by Garrison Keillor.

Looking at the overstuffed mess sitting beside him, Ed Hyman, who had been doing this for longer than I had been alive,
looked at me—half-amused, half-disgusted—and said simply:
"Players . . . travel . . . light." It's a lesson I've never forgotten and
has been reinforced on no shortage of marathon sprints through

airports from London to Los Angeles to Hong Kong and beyond. Of course, it didn't take much time to realize that my camera would do a poor job of discerning the unique essence of a conference room in Cincinnati, from one, let's say, in Boston. The sandwich proved less than useful as well, since the modern airport has become home to food courts so large and wide-ranging in choices that it is difficult to imagine how anyone could go without food or for that matter escape morbid obesity.

Anyway, I think I had a pretty standard reaction to the travel experience. At first, the travel is actually fun and the idea of having to spend an extra hour or two in Dallas doesn't seem all that bad. Within a few years, that two-hour delay seems like a death sentence, especially when you miss your family and those two hours are the difference between spending time with your kids and getting to watch them sleep. The stress of my early years as a salesman accompanying our research analysts was only heightened by the fact that *all* logistical details—addresses, floor numbers, and ground transportation—were our responsibility on a schedule that if managed correctly didn't leave a moment to spare.

And my new bosses were impatient with anyone who failed to make efficient use of travel time. Ed insisted on sitting in coach directly next to his charges so he could make sure we were using the time well. For a guy like me who found a way to turn in *every* term paper in college later than the due date with no consequences, spending ten hours a day sitting next to a nice but serious man who didn't suffer fools lightly was an education, to put it mildly. For the first time in my life, my bullshit couldn't extricate me from being held accountable for my responsibilities to something greater than myself.

It was clear why Ed perennially held that top spot on the *Institutional Investor* list of top economists (his record has now swelled to an incredible thirty-five times, and like DiMaggio's fifty-six-game hitting streak, this is a record that will never be broken, if only for the pure physical stamina such a feat requires). The son of a county clerk in Sweetwater, Texas, Ed is perhaps the most intensely focused and disciplined Wall Street executive I've ever seen. How he manages to keep a sense of humor about himself is beyond me, but he somehow does it. I worked for the man for more than fifteen years, and while I know little about his upbringing, I believe his ascent to the top of the Wall Street game reflects a West Texas type of self-reliance that is increasingly hard to find.

After receiving a degree in engineering from the University of Texas, he went on to earn his MBA from the Sloan School of Management at MIT. He worked for the legendary German-born Harvard economist Otto Eckstein at Data Resources Inc., a company that became the largest nongovernmental distributor of economic data in the world. From there, Ed was hired to be an economist at one of the last great Wall Street research boutiques, C. J. Lawrence, where he eventually rose to the level of vice-chairman. After C. J. merged with Morgan Grenfell and was eventually acquired by Deutsche Bank, Ed decided to start the firm that would give me my first chance. His great business insight was to give customers exactly what they wanted—a revelation for Wall Street research then and now—and he expected the same from us as employees.

Ed never yelled, but he could be the most intimidating little son of a bitch you'd ever meet in your life. One of his favorite techniques was to continue to ask you questions regarding subjects you were required to know well past the point at which it was clear that you were unprepared. As salesmen to some of the largest institutional investors in the world, we were expected to know *everything* about our accounts. Stuffed into economy seats and after ten minutes of pleasantries, a typical interaction might go something like this:

"Why don't you take out a list of your accounts?" he'd say.

"Sure."

"Who's first?"

"ABC Pension."

"How much money do they run?"

I knew this one. "Twenty-five billion dollars."

"Who's the head guy?"

"Jim Smith."

"How do they pay?"

"They have a quarterly vote," I would say confidently. I was on a roll.

Sensing my overconfidence, Ed would then start to throw fastballs on the outside part of the plate. "Where did Jim go to college?"

"Um . . . I'm not sure."

"Do they write a quarterly investment letter?"

"Um . . . yeah, I don't, uh, know."

"What's his assistant's name?"

I just tilted my head, wincing and sucking air through my teeth.

"What's their investment style?"

"Style?"

"Yeah, growth, value, large cap, small cap, what?"

"I haven't gotten that far."

And the questions would continue like that for at least another five minutes until he said, "You know, the salesman at Goldman Sachs would know." He was right and I would nod in glum acceptance, at which point he would ask, "Who's the next account on your list?"

"XYZ Global Advisors."

"OK. Where did the head guy go to college?"

"Dunno." I started to say more quickly, shaking my head and gritting my teeth.

"What's his assistant's name?"

"Not sure."

"Do they write a quarterly investment letter?"

"Gee, Ed, I guess I have a lot more to learn about my accounts."

"Yep," he would say. "Who's the next one on the list?"

"Acme Asset Management."

"Do they write a quarterly investment letter?" And on and on this would continue until the flight ended. This was, to put it nicely, torture. Having woken up at 4:30 a.m. and boarded the plane by 6:00 a.m., I was, by 8:00 a.m., left with virtually no illusions about my self-worth and my place in the industry. This was before any of our client meetings actually started. During these exchanges, there were more than a few occasions when I fantasized faking my own death or hurling myself from the exit doors. This was the big league and no amount of alleged college charm would absolve me from my responsibilities. It didn't take long to learn that I needed to be better prepared. It made for a long day. No stranger to the grape, it was also at this time I discovered alcohol's medicinal qualities to relieve the stress associated with the misery of business travel.

I also started to engage in the time-honored Wall Street tradition of masking one's own insecurities by spending other people's money. Then, as now, Wall Street is largely a variable cost business. This means that when times are good as they were in the early nineties, few people paid any attention to costs, the greater emphasis placed instead on driving high-margin top line. Wall Street may be the only industry I know where you are expected to throw money around and where you can be yelled at for not entertaining clients enough. The practice of using T&E to garner commissions was even more egregious and common before May Day and the advent of negotiated commissions for listed stocks. This epic event occurred on May 1, 1975. In the era preceding that date, whether one bought a hundred or a hundred thousand shares, investors were required to pay the same high fixed commission per share. Few rules and little oversight were employed to dissuade institutional brokers from using their firm's money to entice their clients to direct order flow their way.

By the time I became a salesman in the early 1990s, the egregious uses of "soft dollars" to pay for rent, magazine subscriptions, lunch, and a variety of other operating expenses—that should have been borne by the company—had largely been exposed and rightfully stopped. T&A was and sometimes remains an important part of T&E. Using commissions to pay for research was, thankfully and appropriately, deemed to be acceptable. But while the more distasteful abuses of commissions were frowned upon, they were still widely in use at that time. The expectations to be out and to entertain were, and remain, intense.

There are a number of other Wall Street traditions—like bowler hats and three-martini lunches—that have fallen by the wayside with the march of progress. But the group research luncheon and dinner have forever been staples of the sell-side life, and will likely continue to be. Although they can be quite large affairs, a typical meal with clients will take place in a quiet private room at a high-end restaurant with about twenty people.

When you're in your twenties, and particularly if you didn't grow up rich in a sophisticated city, eating at the world's best restaurants on a regular basis makes you feel like a pro while you're still a rookie. The role of an institutional salesman or securities analyst allows you to eat meals that would be the stuff of pure fantasy if someone else weren't picking up the check. When I stepped into this role in the 1990s, the allure of the haute cuisine of the city's classic French restaurants was still in full force and I often found myself dining several times a week at La Cote Basque,

Lutèce, La Grenouille, and La Caravelle. If there is a problem with money, it is that it is easier to become accustomed to having it than not having it—even if it's not your own. Six months of regularly dining at great restaurants and only the most grounded would find it difficult not to develop a sense of entitlement about both the food and the service of any restaurant.

In the early days of ISI, all of our luncheons in Manhattan were held in the wine cellar at La Cote Basque, which was more or less in our building at 717 Fifth Avenue. We were greeted in French and led through the elegant yet distinctly continental dining room to the stairs leading to the cellar, where we'd nod in acknowledgment at a virtual who's who of the city's power elite.

A fixture in that dining room was a man named Robert Brimberg, otherwise known as Scarsdale Fats, who made a career (and a good one at that) by bringing the best minds on Wall Street together to discuss their favorite stocks over a great meal. His legendary status on the Street was chronicled in Adam Smith's (a nom de plume) wonderful book, *The Money Game:*

> The gentleman who is the Madame de Stael of the institutional investment business is called Scarsdale Fats, and he really does exist. He exists, he gives lunches, and everybody comes. Lunch on Wall Street is working time, and what started at Scarsdale's informally has developed to such a point that the lunch guests bone up beforehand and take notes. On any given day, the lunch guests at Scarsdale's are likely to represent a couple of billion dollars in managed money. Now, when you handle this kind of money, you are, believe me, welcome almost everywhere.*

---

* Adam Smith, *The Money Game*, New York: Vintage Books, 1976, 189.

The ideas he picked up from those get-togethers would be turned into research and after a while an invitation to one was an important sign that you had arrived in the upper echelons of finance. Regrettably, I never got to know Fats or attend one of his famed luncheons. But with the encouragement of his son, Fred, a friend and client, we occasionally host our own.

Our affairs at ISI were somewhat more formal. After fifteen minutes of pleasantries, we would all sit down around one oval table, and the ritual was as predictable as Catholic Mass. Ed would start by introducing himself and asking his guests to fill out a quick survey of their thoughts on the market. Then he proceeded to have everyone introduce themselves, moving clockwise. Good (or extremely good, for those who could tell the difference, which seemed to be just about everyone but me) wines were served, and there was virtually no interaction between the waitstaff and the assorted guests.

While this ritual still exists on Wall Street, it has been shortened from well over two hours to less than an hour and a half. In another change, few people drink alcohol of any sort during the day. The business is just too competitive these days to take too much time or dim your senses. But back then, everyone knew the routine. Their quiet professionalism ensured that—after what must have been thousands of such encounters before my shadow darkened Wall Street—there would be no distractions from the business at hand. The meal started either with asparagus or salad, the entrée was always fish at lunch and perhaps something special like rack of lamb at dinner, and for dessert something sensible like berries with crème fraîche. Chicken, we were warned, was too déclassé to serve to clients.

In my early twenties, I was still hopelessly new to the concept of eating at high-end restaurants. Such a happy occasion occurred only rarely while I was growing up: let's say, on my mom's birthday. Invariably, my dad's attempts at chivalry would be thwarted when my mother, spotting the prices of the entrées, couldn't help herself and ordered something like a grilled cheese sandwich. It was such a source of embarrassment for all concerned (with the exception of my mother) that if we ate out at all, it was almost always at the Candlelight Diner on Veterans Highway in Commack. I still eat there with my mom. It's a clean, well-lighted place, but you'll never find a review of it in Zagat.

I should have learned the basics of client lunches from the effortless presentations at La Cote Basque, but I still possessed a childlike vision of what it was like to "live large." What few choices we had as salesmen to influence the meal were completely ruined by my decision at a luncheon I hosted in Charlotte, after which no one dared suggest diversion from the accepted conventions. I was twenty-three at the time and, given my first big chance to "shoot the works" with someone else's dough, I wound up choosing an adolescent's idea of what haute cuisine was supposed to be: shrimp cocktail, prime rib (rare of course), and apple pie à la mode.

Looking back at it now, I realize that Ed must have been embarrassed in front of his clients the same way my father was embarrassed in front of the waitstaff when my mom ordered that grilled cheese sandwich. It was one of the few times in the early years that I remember Ed being visibly angry with me. Back in New York a day later, he called me into his office and said bluntly, "Look, if I eat what you ordered for lunch yesterday at every meal, I'm going to be dead before I'm fifty. From now on, it's salad, fish, and berries. No exceptions. Let the other salesmen know." It was in this way that my gaucherie became the provenance of one of the least popular rules for salesmen at ISI. I have been the "salad, fish, and berries" guy ever since.

Like everything else in today's society, the group luncheon or dinner has become somewhat less formal. This is partly because of the growth in the hedge fund industry, whose denizens don't like to wear suits and ties to work and, generally speaking, eschew what they see as the time-wasting pretensions found at the great restaurants during business hours. It is also rare to find people who drink alcohol, even wine, during the day. More than twenty years later, I'm convinced that the group meal is almost atavistic to the inner workings of commerce. The word "company" itself derives from the Latin *cum panis*. For thousands of years it seems merchants and other businessmen would discuss their future plans over a meal, "with bread."

There are the meetings at fancy hotels and restaurants, and there are the meetings at offices around the country. In attendance at each of them will be the quirky colleagues with high opinions of themselves and clients who may be even more impressed with their own genius. As it is with most things in life, I find that the most talented often have the fewest pretensions. Being an effective institutional salesman on Wall Street requires an almost perfect blend of both humility and commercial aggressiveness. Memories of my early meetings and pitches often wash over me at the oddest times today when, more than twenty years later, I am the one the salesman thinks is just a little too demanding and glib. There was the charmer whose only two responses to any investment thesis were "next" (always issued diffidently, midsentence) and "tell me more." You only knew the meeting was over with him when he completely started to ignore you and began to refocus solely on the screen before him. The only thing he didn't do to complete the picture of self-important Wall Street jerk was take his own blood pressure, Gordon Gekko–style, during your prepared remarks.

After three or four such meetings, my self-esteem threshold lengthened to four or five minutes—any less than that and I felt that I was weak, any more, that I possessed the charm of Dean

Martin and the investment acumen of Benjamin Graham. A less obnoxious and more effective version of this approach has been adopted by a successful mutual fund that insists that none of its portfolio managers or analysts ask any questions or provide any nonverbal cues of agreement or disagreement during presentations until the sell-side analyst has finished recounting his best ideas. The basis of this practice is the idea that sell-side analysts are too eager to please and often shade their views, consciously or subconsciously, to fit those of their hosts. It's a good idea but it requires more self-control than you might think. Having tried this myself, I'd say that it also kind of takes the fun out of it.

All Wall Street firms do the circuit to some degree, whether it's to take corporate clients or the firm's own analysts around to visit institutional investors, and some of the characters we rely upon to help us make these trips—the car service drivers in particular—know more about the financial industry than many of their slick clients from New York. Perhaps the best embodiment of this was a limousine driver named Larry from Pittsburgh.

Larry was without pretense, nobody's fool, and spoke his mind. He also had the kind of offbeat sense of humor one only finds between the wiseass coasts of America. He was in his early fifties, with thinning blond hair. His late-model Lincoln was spotless and smelled brand-new, he was impeccably dressed, and he had few qualms about sharing what he learned from the other Wall Street road shows that employed his services. On more than one occasion he scooped the wire services on Street news. "Lehman's going to lay off their emerging markets desk next week," or "I hear Mack is coming back to Morgan Stanley." He was also a relentless gossip and used the slightest lull in conversation to deliver honest and often outrageously funny observations about some of the people who rode in the back of his car. He wouldn't be afraid to tell you that the famous biotech analyst at Merrill had "the worst breath in the business" or that the CEO of Lehman was "nuttier than a fruitcake."

He was a favorite of institutional salesmen across the country because he was unafraid of the Wall Street titans and corporate chieftains riding in the backseat of his car. He was long past the point where he would tolerate being pushed around. In one famous story, he got into a tangle with one of Wall Street's most high-powered female executives. She was heir to one of those most irritating traits of important people—the proclivity to second-guess other people, often experts, on subjects about which she knew nothing and with which she had no experience.

She rubbed Larry the wrong way from the beginning. Her handler from the company had to take it, but Larry—God bless him—did not. She regularly terrorized hotel concierges, limousine drivers, and anyone she perceived was an obstacle to her getting precisely what she wanted at the moment she wanted it. Lord have mercy on the poor soul of the man who had to drive her if her BlackBerry or her phone was not working. She heckled them mercilessly:

"Do you know the right way to go?"

"Why did you take this road? It has so much traffic."

"Can you turn the heat down?"

"Can you turn the radio to Bloomberg News?"

Most of the drivers were accustomed to such types and took her chiding in stride. But Larry was a professional and he wasn't about to "take any shit from some dame" in a St. John knit dress. He had seen executives come and go and he correctly surmised that his career would last longer than theirs. Unable to take one of this financial diva's seemingly endless litanies of complaints and suggestions, he angrily stopped his car so abruptly that her body was thrown forward into the back of the passenger seat with an ignominious *ba-dum* that must have hurt.

"Until today," he bellowed with the dramatic flair of a Southern Baptist minister, "Sumner Redstone was the most annoying person to ever set foot in this car, but you now hold that title. Why don't you do your job, lady, and I'll do mine?"

She was shocked. People simply did not talk to her that way. Speechless, she started to twirl her hair and sulk. The young investment banking associate traveling with her could hardly contain his amusement and pleasure at someone sticking it to the man and proceeded to tell just about everyone he ever met on Wall Street about it. While Larry lost her business, he more than made up for it with business from other Wall Street guys who heard the story and loved it. When you spend your life on the road, you have to appreciate the little things.

In all my travels to visit our clients on the sell side, there was one regular meeting with a quirky midwestern fellow that always stood out. He worked for an enormous mutual fund outfit in the breadbasket of America and had achieved great success as an investor and a fiduciary over a long period of time. He was in his late sixties when I first met him and was anachronistically thin for a businessman. You were always escorted to a chair in front of his desk while he looked out the large picture window behind it. Without turning he would launch into what seemed an interminable and almost always incomprehensible monologue on his views of the markets and the economy, the relative merits of a variety of agricultural capital goods, or whatever happened to be on his mind at the time.

Without warning, he would ask a question that often had nothing to do with the subject at hand. "What's your favorite consumer product and why?" His tolerance for bullshit was zero and his steely blue eyes let you know that an insufficient answer could lead to a very short meeting.

If you passed the first test he'd then ask you to indicate what the last two trades you made in your personal account happened to be. He thought the answers to those questions could more quickly get to the heart of what an analyst really believed without leafing through a thirty-page handout.

He was an important customer (and he knew it), and though he was firm, he was never rude—just intimidating. He became somewhat famous in sell-side circles when he forced an *Institutional Investor*–ranked sell-side analyst covering Eastman Kodak to admit, rather sheepishly, that he had never owned a camera. It was at that point that he unceremoniously had security usher the offending analyst out of the building and onto the sidewalk. One of the ironies of the investment business these days is that sell-side securities analysts are often prevented from owning any of the companies they follow.

While this may seem appealing in the wake of the scandals that wracked the investment business in the late nineties, it's hard not to believe we've lost something important, and maybe even fun, in our attempts to sanitize what will always be a risky business. Being able to invest in the very stocks you "discover" and tell your clients about was for many years one of the great joys of being a sell-side analyst. Of course, the inscrutable found ways to use their platform for their own gain against the best interests of their clients, so now many analysts can't personally buy or sell any of the companies they cover.

Even the friendliest meetings with good-natured clients involve some modicum of stress, and after six or seven meetings in a single day, only the most stoic among us have the desire to go back to their hotel room and work out or learn a foreign language or engage in some other productive and life-affirming exercise. Nope, at that point, you feel an almost insatiable desire to reward yourself. You've been up since the middle of the night,

you've had very little fun, you've had to be perpetually charming, and whatever cultural or tourist sites exist in the burg you
happen to be in at the moment have long since closed. For me,
this often left as a recreational option only the hotel bar, where
I'd invariably find my colleagues and knock a few back and have
some laughs.

The desultory nature of the travel also rendered it difficult to
establish much of a routine. My wife would often joke that I traveled to both the best and the worst places in no particular order.
While one week you might find yourself visiting Paris and walking along the Seine on your way to eat alone at a local bistro, the
next week you might find yourself in, say, Omaha. In Omaha your
choices for nighttime recreation are considerably less robust. Your
inner gourmand has to satisfy itself with steak or, if it must have
something ethnic, take a leap of faith that usually results in bitter
disappointment. While the fancy-pants hotel in Chicago might
boast a spa replete with an executive men's facial, a pool, and a gym,
the Embassy Suites in Fargo is a bit more cut-and-dried. There,
instead of being greeted on arrival with a large bowl of polished
green apples and mango-pomegranate iced tea, you'll find a vend-
ing machine. But there was almost always a bar.

Later, when I read the biography of Bill Wilson, founder of
Alcoholics Anonymous, I was not shocked to learn that he had
been a securities analyst in the 1920s. He was paid to travel from
town to town across the vast expanse of America to find companies that were underappreciated and unloved. Perhaps unsurprisingly, his success only seemed to feed his addiction to alcohol.
"Meanwhile the drinking was going up and up and up, but I was
making so goddamn much money and that was a symbol of importance, and I was Mr. Big, and I was in the big-time speculator
clique as their number-one investigator, so what the hell! Do you

see?"* His understanding of the business traveler's problem apparently allowed him to found an organization that would serve many on Wall Street.

Given the popularity of the hotel bar, it quickly became apparent to me why Bibles can be found in every hotel room in America. The temptations aren't that great in, let's say, Des Moines, but they can be greater in the kinds of towns that specialize in temptation. Yes, a life on the road is filled with temptations and bad habits—none of them constructive. If you're lucky, as I was, the bad habits you develop are merely illicit and not illegal. The illicit habits, especially the drinking, can be just as destructive, but hopefully they won't prompt you to have to call one of your traveling companions in the middle of the night to bail you out of jail.

Having grown up watching movies in which a captured glance across a crowded room inevitably led to romance between strangers, I often found myself looking for such opportunities on the road. Spend a couple of nights on the road alone and lonely, and you'd be forgiven, single or married, for fantasizing about the prospects for romance, or at the very least sex. But after thousands of such nights, I can report that the opportunities for such dalliances are painfully rare if they exist at all. In all my years, I've never seen a young, attractive woman with fewer problems than I had ever sidle up to a hotel bar. The crowd is predictably comprised of other lonely men or groups of businessmen and women together for some conference. The people in groups obviously have a lot more fun. The lone men, if they are unable to find trouble, content themselves with hard liquor, cashews from the minibar, and cinematic classics like *Nancy, Yvonne, and What the Parrot Saw.*

---

* Bill Wilson, *Bill W.: My First 40 Years: An Autobiography by the Cofounder of Alcoholics Anonymous*, Hazelden Publishing, 1954.

And as noted at the beginning of this chapter, the pretty stewardesses of the early days of commercial airline travel have been replaced largely by bitter unionized termagants working for bankrupt companies, and the jet-set passengers have been replaced by guys in shorts or leopard-print sweat pants at any time of year and in any part of the plane. Once you spend a night in one of the "cities" in the vast expanse of America, the purple neon lights of gentlemen's clubs might also beckon, at which point any attempt to attain the metaphysical gifts of faith, hope, and charity might be replaced by the attentions of Faith, Hope, and Charity—all aspiring medical students, by the way. More than twenty years later, I'm still hoping to run into a doctor, or even a nurse, that ever looked anything like these girls, and such is the pity. It's a novel form of entertainment when you're in your twenties, but it doesn't take long to learn that this is a complete waste of time and money and will never fill the forever empty.

The loneliness of the road can produce other kinds of behavior—for example the wanton use of a company expense account. Some people have jobs that actually require them to work outdoors and break a sweat—jobs that require physical labor and that usually pay very little. People on Wall Street, despite the fact that they often get paid handsomely for pushing paper around, often respond to the pressure to produce by thinking their employers are screwing them and whatever they're getting paid is not enough. After all, what kind of industry would pay Smithers enough to buy a five-bedroom summer house in Spring Lake while all you've been able to afford is that dinky three-bedroom in Sea Girt? I work hard, don't I? Damn straight. I deserve it, don't I? You betcha. No one's going to notice this $145 expense in the traffic accident that is my hotel bill, will they? Not on your life. The Swedish massage, the executive facial, and renting *Die Hard 4* at three in the morning would never be caught and, even if they were, would probably be ignored if you were producing.

Despite the stresses of the road, my early days at ISI were among the best years of my career. In addition to the friendships and camaraderie and opportunities to learn, I was exposed to some of the greatest minds in the investment business and started to read voraciously anything I could get my hands on. My colleagues and I became great friends and had the kind of fun reserved for people in their twenties. Once we were off the clock, we had no responsibilities. We also started to make some real money, which was nice but hardly the panacea we had envisioned. The problem with money, as I was to find out, is that it's relative. There is a natural human tendency to get accustomed very quickly to whatever you're getting paid and to start to assume a level of respect that is incongruent to your station in the industry or in life. For a guy who never stayed at a hotel any better than a Holiday Inn growing up, I found myself becoming apoplectic if a complimentary fruit basket didn't happen to be delivered to my room at the Four Seasons. For a twenty-four-year-old spending other people's money, such churlishness was a little rich.

Starting to make some money also launched the almost unstoppable process of settling on the "number" at which you could relax, be happy, and finally start to enjoy life. "If I could only make a hundred thousand a year" quickly became "If I could only make two hundred thousand a year" and so on, until it became clear, years later, that money was a poor substitute for happiness. While money eliminates many of life's inconveniences, it could never fully take the place of pride, self-respect, and peace of mind when it came to the important things.

The greater irony is that once you start to use money as a measure of success versus others in Manhattan, you are destined to be depressed. There will always be someone with more money, especially in the great metropolis that is New York. It has always been thus, but it is never difficult to find some dope on Wall Street who makes a lot more money than you do and there are few places (except perhaps Hollywood) where it is more apparent that God doesn't sign paychecks and that life is unfair. My first bonus at ISI, in 1992, was $37,500. It was big money then—and now for that matter—for a guy in his early twenties. It was roughly equivalent to my base salary. I was so in debt and had struggled financially for so long that I stood up, clapped my hands, and said excitedly to Ed, "Is this in pesos? This is great! Thank you, thank you, thank you!" I wasn't much of a poker player. Two years later, when my bonuses were larger, I had sadly become accustomed to them, was never satisfied, and made a mistake that ultimately became a blessing in disguise.

In those early days, I became friendly with a portfolio manager named Dino who ran a small money management shop for his mostly Italian American client base. Our common heritage became the basis for a great friendship. He was a good client and we had a lot of laughs. One day, he urged me to take a look at "investing" in a company out of Ho-Ho-Kus, New Jersey. He was convinced that the CEO, a friend of his, had developed a diagnostic tool that would rival the CAT scan at a fraction of the price. It couldn't miss, and I had a chance to get in on the ground floor. And so I found myself, at twenty-five, writing a check to the personal bank account of the firm's founder—this in spite of the fact that this guy who claimed to be a doctor of medicine possessed an almost shocking disregard for his own health and hygiene.

This was my quick ticket to riches without hard work. After the whole thing was revealed to be a colossal scam, the other suckers and I retained separate legal counsel. Some sued, but my lawyer, a slightly older classmate from Georgetown with wisdom beyond his years, told me to forget it. He thought I should consider the whole affair a form of what he called *rebbe gelt*—a Yiddish term for "money you learn from." He explained that the $30,000 would pale in comparison to the money I would save by avoiding investments in other "sure things" when I actually had some degree of sustainable wealth later on in life.

As it turned out, my aborted quick trip to a life of foreign automobiles and mysterious women hastened my decision to get smarter. I would ultimately go for my MBA. It was clear that I wasn't nearly as smart as I thought I was. Unfortunately, my adventure also seriously depleted the funds I was to use for graduate school, leading to two long years of Cup-a-Soup and meaningful debts upon graduation.

But those sacrifices seemed worth it. In the early 1990s, as today, the big-money guys were all hedge fund types. Having covered many of the best funds at the time, I knew that I didn't have the training to switch over to the buy side as so many people on the sell side wished to do in those days.

Ultimately, I reverted to the choice of doing what was expected and safe from the standpoint of my peers: I applied to business school with a romantic vision of someday becoming a great *speculator*. Ed, who had an MBA from MIT himself, knew enough to believe that I was making a mistake and said so. Why leave the kind of prestigious, great-paying job so many people go to business school to get in the first place, he asked. Still, he didn't stand in my way, understanding that the value of youth lies in making its own mistakes.

4

"B" SCHOOL

On the occasion of the tenth Christmas season after my graduation from business school, one of the broad-assed type A's from my "cohort" managed to find my e-mail address and implored me and all the other unlucky recipients of her efficiency to "share our experiences and successes in the ten years that had gone by since we were all together." Taking great pains to accidentally use the Reply All function, a classmate named Miguel told us of his efforts to form a union-free bottling company in his native Mexico. Brad informed us that the best thing about his family life was "everything" and that, oh, incidentally, he had made managing director last summer, not realizing or caring that these two concepts were so incongruous as to be laughable to anyone remotely familiar with the workings of an investment bank. Suzanne had formed a consulting firm and had twins. And on it went, each life update sickeningly more perfect than the last, a series of lies passed along as some form of rationalization of the truth.

It had been ten years, during which I had little contact with these people with the exception of my similarly cynical, honest, and funny friends Steve Hadley and John Barker. But I can't say that I wasn't curious about whether my classmates had gained more perspective since the days when we were all pursuing our MBAs. It was one of those mornings between Christmas and New Year's when all but the most junior Wall Streeters were able to get away to Vail or to St. Bart's or to take time off, stay in the city, and spend a little of their bonuses. I was in the latter camp, and trying desperately to suppress my growing anger at each new monument to pretension.

Although I knew better than to be offended by the dick measuring that came to typify interactions with other business-school types from Wharton, Harvard, and Stanford, Ashish's short bio enraged me. "Although I don't have to work since selling my two start-ups to venture capital funds in the late 1990s, I am currently working on Sand Hill Road helping to provide capital to companies trying to solve the 'last mile' problem. I am happily living with my wife and family in Northern California, where I just decided to roll the dice on a 5,000-square-foot home in Palo Alto. Wish me luck!" After reading this, the only thing I was wishing for Ashish and his new manse was an act of God for which he had no insurance. As usual, my fallback position when confronted with the indignities associated with people yearning to impress was petulance and vain attempts at humor. So I responded with my own life-affirming update.

"Yes, it is so nice to hear from everyone!" I began. "Unfortunately, I have not been as lucky as you all have been although things are looking up now. I had a few good years during the Bubble but my life really took a turn for the worse with the SEC investigation. I then got mixed up with prescription drugs after I got my wisdom teeth taken out in 2001. (Who knew hydrocodone was addictive?) But I've managed to get through Hazelden and my second divorce relatively unscathed emotionally and I've met a wonderful girl (she's only 16!) from a mail-order service out of the Philippines. The authorities say I might have to adopt her before we tie the knot but that's a story for another day. The good news is that despite some of these setbacks I have been able to raise $500 million for my long/short global macro hedge fund with a currency overlay. I figure I just might need one good year and then I'm outta here. All the best to everyone and stay in touch!"

I hoped that turning my anger into petulance might somehow magically boost the efficacy of the three Advil I'd popped upon waking up. "Same old Jase" most must have thought, the irrepressible wiseass and business school cynic. There were undoubtedly others who could only hope that my briefing was accurate, allowing them to be smug and show pity at the same time, while notching another marker in their climb to corporate success.

Seventeen years later I still often wonder what I was thinking when I decided to ignore Ed Hyman's advice and leave a good-paying job at a great firm to go to business school in the middle of a bull market. Mystifyingly dumb, I had convinced myself that I didn't have the academic background necessary to compete in a world of ever-accelerating financial modernization. Admittedly, my decision to attend business school was due in equal measure to the comfort of conformity and to my romantic nature. I am not exaggerating when I say that I thought I was about to enter a club wherein all the secrets of America's captains of industry would be revealed to me. I assumed that the spirits of J. P. Morgan and Vanderbilt and Carnegie would seep into the fabric of the place and into my studies.

My delusions about what took place at America's business schools were quickly dashed after attending math camp, after enduring team-building exercises replete with trust falls in the Poconos, and after eating my first meal at the Anvil Club, a place I had imagined to be a leather-couched salon in which pipe-smoking professors with elbow patches discussed the weighty issues of fiscal and monetary policy and international trade. Only after my first meal there did I realize that it was just like any other public institution cafeteria and that a professor from an elite MBA program wouldn't eat there on a bet.

The most troubling thing about my unfortunate life decision was this: business school is really more of an expensive placement agency for would-be industrialists and financiers than it is an institution of higher learning. It was frustrating for me because I'd just left an enviable job, and underscored by the fact that the recruiting process at a place like Wharton starts *the very first day* of classes.

Before my very first class on my very first day of business school, one of the students in my cohort stood up in front of us in Corporate Finance, introduced himself, and then attempted to sell us all lanyards for our ID cards for the "low, low price of three dollars." A little later that day, I went to a recruiting presentation for Lehman Brothers. As luck would have it, the speaker was none other than its chairman, Dick Fuld. "Not all of you are cut out for this business. Our interview process will ferret you out," he thundered, the vein on the side of his temple almost bursting under the strain of his passion for the business and for his firm. An old high school girlfriend worked in the recruiting office at Lehman, and I was able to catch up with her after Mr. Fuld's performance.

"Jeanine, I'm not sure I would lead with Dick as a recruiting technique. Half the guys in the room are going home to change their shorts now," I chided.

"I know. Alec and I try to dissuade him from coming but he insists on being involved with recruiting the 'next generation.'"

And so, while it feels like an eternity ago, it seems as if my first day of business school was punctuated by the performances of two salesmen, one a rookie, the other a veteran, but both obnoxious harbingers of the period of excess that was to ensue. The recruiting process, I was to learn, was really the raison d'être of the place and the focus of my entire tenure on Walnut Street. First-year MBAs spend their entire time searching for an internship between the first and second years, and the second year they spend their entire time trying to convert that internship into a full-time job. Impromptu gatherings of students and professors to discuss the weighty issues of international economics and finance are non-existent and seen correctly, I believe, as a waste of time given the exigencies of paying off one's student debt upon graduation.

In yet another odd feature of what I thought was to be the hallowed ground of American capitalism, the focus on recruiting was, perhaps unintentionally, made greater by the school's "grade non-disclosure policy." As students in a school designed putatively to celebrate the merits of free markets and competition, we were made to vow, with no sense of irony, not to disclose our grades or our class rank to would-be employers during the recruiting process. The thinking behind the edict was that the MBA class represented a wide variety of academic backgrounds and that some who had majored in business during their undergraduate years would have an unfair advantage due to their work experience or undergraduate studies in the more rigorous accounting and finance classes.

As someone trained by one of Wall Street's best economists, it took me about thirty seconds upon learning of the policy to conclude that the most efficient use of my time at business school would be to do the bare minimum to pass my classes and graduate while spending far more of my time on the recruiting process. Most of the students pursuing a career in finance quickly came to the same conclusion. The only ones who didn't seem to go along were the management consulting students who for whatever reason were still obsessed with being "smarter" than everyone else.

(To be fair, many of the management consulting firms recruiting on campus found creative ways to intuit a potential recruit's grades. It was not uncommon for a twenty-eight-year-old MBA student, for instance, to be asked what his SAT scores had been a decade before.)

If this wasn't enough to make everyone wish to mail it in on their studies, the forced grading curve was another strong incentive to do as little as possible. Sixty-five percent of the class was to receive the grade of Pass, 25 percent were given a High Pass, and the top 10 percent were given the banal distinction of Distinguished Service. Of the sixteen classes I took at Wharton, I received two High Passes, no DS's, and only narrowly averted a failing grade in Securities Law. Given the academic skills of my classmates, the effort required to turn a Pass into a High Pass was simply not worth it, especially given the fact that it would be considered unethical to reveal your grades.

This may sound harsh and perhaps it is. My frame of mind wasn't aided in any way by the fact that I missed New York and the girl who was eventually to become my wife. Any great desire to study on my own was also washed away by the realization that I was better off spending my time looking for a job than truly expanding my horizons intellectually.

In all, I would say that about a year of the two years was actually worthwhile. The real basics were the things you would remember the rest of your life: corporate finance, financial and cost accounting, statistics, marketing, and most important now that I look back at it, organizational behavior. The greatest benefit to attending a place like Wharton was meeting some of its professors—like the acclaimed Jeremy Siegel, an expert on the financial markets—and the almost never-ending parade of luminaries from the business world who regularly lectured on campus. Having the opportunity to sit down and listen to legendary real estate investor Sam Zell, Wall Street legend Marty Zweig, former director of White House protocol in the Kennedy administration Letitia Baldrige, or even the infamous Michael Milken were among the most fascinating and useful experiences I had while I was at business school.

For all the pretensions of being a "business" school, which implies that some of its graduates might actually wind up in operating businesses that produce things like automobiles, pharmaceuticals, or even soap, the stark reality is that the vast majority of graduates from elite MBA programs seek remora-fish-type jobs in investment banking or management consulting because they sport the gaudiest entry-level salaries. In fairness, Harvard, Wharton, or Chicago never overtly push their students into such careers. The intense competition for them is driven primarily by the vast out-of-pocket and opportunity costs of leaving jobs to attend graduate school, and secondarily the atavistic competitiveness and lack of imagination of the average business school student. (I was an enthusiastic example of both phenomena.) A friend of mine once told me that some of the dumbest people he had ever met were at Harvard Law School. It sounds like a ridiculous statement, but I knew immediately what he meant.

Virtually all of the people that attend elite business schools are academically gifted and have unusual drive and ambition. But aside from the guys who came out of the military, many of us also have virtually no perspective on life and lack the most basic interest in humanity when we perceived the stakes to be so high. Life to some of us becomes a game measured not in money but in prestige, a currency that has virtually no practical use. My years at Wharton stood as a testament to Keynes's observation that most men would rather fail conventionally than risk succeeding unconventionally.

One of the greatest ironies of the business school recruiting process is that those who are characterized as losers in the jobs sweepstakes often wind up being the biggest winners immediately after graduation. The "losers" are generally thought to be those who are either uninterested or unable to get jobs at high-profile companies through the recruiting office. Funnily enough, while those who take the road less traveled can't seem to impress lithe co-eds while they're in school, they often have virtually limitless access to them once they are in the business world.

One of the best examples of this phenomenon is a friend by the name of Jim Bankoff. It's such a compelling example of the vagaries of the recruiting process that I often recount his story to undergraduate and graduate students who feel that getting a job at Goldman Sachs will solve all their problems and, financially, set them up for life. Jim was a smart, polite kid with a perpetually bemused expression on his face who spent his undergraduate years at Emory University in Atlanta. Jim was no different than the rest of us, I suppose, except that he was preternaturally kind and perhaps too laid-back to convince the true believers who hosted on-campus interviews that he had the fire in the belly required to become a corporate killer. Jim received a few offers in his chosen field, management consulting—which for some reason still unknown to me took itself more seriously than investment banking—but was blanked at the top-tier firms like McKinsey, Boston Consulting Group, and Bain. This led him to rely on companies and contacts outside the normal on-campus channels.

For all the self-important talk of being trailblazers in the business community, there were few things more embarrassing to the business school student in the midnineties than to take a job with a company no one had ever heard of or—ye gods, worse—to be unemployed or undecided about your future upon graduation. The expense of time and money associated with an MBA made such a "failure" utterly shameful or, if the result of the student's personal choice, outright heretical. Candidly, we all felt a little sorry for Jim, often offering patronizing words of encouragement to him on his quest for positions at companies other MBA students at elite programs would never remotely consider.

After some research, Jim became intrigued with a then-little-known company in Arlington, Virginia, and one of its top executives, Steve Case. Given that this was 1996, a point at which the Internet boom was in its infancy, it was decidedly unimpressive for him to be seeking a job with an Internet service provider. But Jim saw the potentially transformative nature of the work and contacted the company's human resources department to set up an informational interview. Hopeful, he boarded a train from Philadelphia's Thirtieth Street station on a cold February morning, arriving in Virginia three hours later only to discover that the human resources department had mistakenly scheduled the appointment for the wrong day. Disappointed and disillusioned, Jim walked around the company's campus in a daze, important questions about his future hanging as heavy as the gloaming settling on the Potomac as evening approached. Was business school really the guarantee of success everyone seemed to think it was? Had all the sacrifices over the last two years been worth it? Had his parents already rented out his room?

By happenstance, he saw a pack of chalk-striped executives walking his way. On a whim and figuring he had little to lose, he approached the man who appeared to lead the pack, extended his hand, and said, "I'm a Wharton MBA and I'd like to work for you." Perhaps too surprised or too humane to rebuff such a fresh-faced suitor, the executive said, without breaking stride, "OK, kid, you've got five minutes to tell me why I should hire you." Jim proceeded to tell the then-unknown executive about his education and his dreams and his values.

The rest, as they say, is history. As it turned out, the VIP he met near dusk was the legendary Ted Leonsis, the founder of America Online, serial entrepreneur, and the current owner of both the NHL's Washington Capitals and the NBA's Washington Wizards. The guy we all felt so sorry for because of his failure to land a post at Bain or McKinsey had just talked himself into a job that would take him, by almost providential luck, into the C-suite level of a firm that would be among the most influential in the Internet boom that was to follow. By 1999, a mere three years after his chance encounter, Jim became the company's executive vice-president of Programming and Products, developing a wide range of groundbreaking Web sites including AOL.com, MapQuest, Moviefone, AOL Music, Netscape, and AOL Instant Messenger. He went on to establish TMZ, FanHouse, BloggingStocks, and Edgadget and is now chairman and CEO of Vox Media and a senior advisor for Providence Equity Partners. As you can imagine, he still sports that bemused expression.

By any objective measure—prestige, responsibility, money—the smart but humble kid everyone felt sorry for in business school became the most immediately and eminently successful of Wharton's 1996 MBA class. To me, he was also the human embodiment of the notion that MBA programs in those days, with their relentless focus on finding jobs at traditional prestige companies, did a wonderful job of producing middle managers but a poor job of training self-motivated innovators and would-be entrepreneurs.

I've also found that for whatever reason newly minted MBAs become obsessed with status over actual achievement, more concerned about being immediately recognized as successful by nature of where they work than by the quality and potential of the position they actually have. Being recognized as "smart" becomes more important than money—an odd ambition for a true capitalist. This is really pretty silly because, let's face it, derivatives traders and management consultants aren't exactly splitting atoms or performing complex spinal cord surgeries in the course of their working days. And yet, the charade that what MBAs do for a living requires extraordinary intellectual capabilities continues.

In the world of the financial markets, this misplaced self-confidence has grown substantially with the growth of hedge funds and alternative investment vehicles and their outsized returns during the bear market. Perhaps it's necessary to justify a 20 percent cut of the profits, but there are more than a few young hedge fund analysts I've met who insist they were actually correct and the market was wrong when they lost money on their positions in 2003. It's as if they believe their clients award them style points if the thought process behind a losing position was sufficiently sophisticated, nuanced, and abstruse.

A famous study about Harvard Business School graduates found that its students would rarely chart their own career choices and, generally speaking, followed the herd into industries that were just about to peak. In 1987, Harvard Business School grads desperately wanted to enter the merger and acquisition boom on Wall Street. Then came October 1987 and the crash. In 1989, it was real estate's turn to crash. In 2000, it was Internet start-ups that crashed and burned. This study is important because it suggests that "smart," educated people are just as likely to succumb to the vicissitudes and whims of crowd behavior as other mere mortals. This obviously rings true to anyone who worked on Wall Street or in Silicon Valley in the late 1990s. This sentiment was captured perfectly in what many consider the seminal work on the subject of crowd behavior, Gustave Le Bon's *The Crowd: A Study on the Popular Mind:*

> In the case of everything that belongs to the realm of sentiment—religion, politics, morality, the affections and antipathies, etc.—the eminent men seldom surpass the standard

of the most ordinary individuals. From the intellectual point of view an abyss may exist between a great mathematician and his boot-maker, but from the point of view of character, the difference is often slight or nonexistent.

There is no real antidote to blindly following the consensus except a curious mixture of humility and self-confidence that has been a consistent and reliable hallmark of great investors. Ultimately no one in the financial markets really cares how smart you are. Performance, and performance alone, equals smarts in our business. The market is always right. As a new entrepreneur and a strategist during the financial crisis that followed the housing bust, I have had a lot of time to think about business school in the last eight years, when one by one many of the basic academic financial orthodoxies I learned there have been almost completely discredited. They include the ideas that:

1. Debt is always cheaper than equity. There is obviously some logic to this, especially in periods of stable interest rates and growing earnings. Add inflation and tax considerations into the mix, and the decision to use debt as a form of capital is even easier, as prices rise and debts can be paid with even cheaper dollars while interest expense becomes tax deductible. Like a lot of modern economic theories that rely more on mathematics than common sense, this financing technique works extremely well until it stops working, at which time it fails spectacularly. In periods of deflation and weaker economic growth, the fixed nature of interest payments becomes a very difficult burden to bear. A greater reliance on the *great moderation* of economic cyclicality and an arrogant belief that cash flows could be consistently and accurately predicted allowed many modern financiers to feel comfortable with leverage ratios of 30:1.

2. Financial markets are generally efficient. This old chestnut came to us courtesy of Eugene Fama of the University of Chicago and generally asserts that financial markets are informationally efficient: reflecting all known information. To be fair, my professors at business school always offered up intellectual trapdoors of the "weak," "semistrong," and "strong" forms of the efficient market theory to allow all of us to hold on to an academically popular orthodoxy despite an almost overwhelming amount of evidence to the contrary. The thinking was that if you put enough monkeys in front of a typewriter, one of them would come up with *War and Peace*. George Soros and Julian Robertson were really just two examples of extraordinarily lucky coin flippers. Right—whatever. While few would quibble with the idea that the sheer amount of information available to investors today makes true information arbitrage ever more difficult to achieve, the re-emergence of government policy on business and financial market decisions as well as the internationalization of the global economy will provide fresh opportunities for investors willing to do their homework.

3. Modern Portfolio Theory (MPT) works when you want it to. Pioneered by Harry Markowitz in his paper "Portfolio Selection," published in 1952 by the *Journal of Finance*, MPT holds that it is possible to construct an "efficient frontier" of optimal portfolios that allow investors to use diverse assets to provide stable returns given a certain level of risk. Again, this theory can work pretty well in periods of stability, but fails miserably in times of intense stress. In some ways, that makes the theory more dangerous than no theory at all, a little bit like how David Einhorn described the concept of value at risk (VAR) as an airbag that works perfectly until you have a car accident. The problem with MPT is that it ignores the impact of liquidity on correlations between asset classes. In plain English, it fails to recognize that in times of market stress investors will sell both good assets and bad assets in equal measure. In fact, the higher quality assets will be sold first if only because there is actually some interest in buying them. When you can't sell what you want, the old saying goes, you sell what you can. This was especially true in 2008, when the correlations of most asset classes all converged on one. In the future, pensions and endowments are most likely to suffer the consequences of a theory that led to the widespread adoption of the "Yale model" and its advocacy of an overallocation to illiquid alternative asset classes.

4. *Home prices always appreciate.* "They ain't making any more of it," every real estate speculator proclaimed to anyone within earshot before the bottom fell out. This one is a little harder to pin on the academic community, as it was put forth by so many market prognosticators (myself included) that it entered the realm of conventional wisdom, just shy of the imprimatur of academic theory. It was also empirically true for nearly seventy years. Certainly, we aren't making more land, but we greatly increased, through financial wizardry and social engineering, the number of those willing to extend home loans to people that couldn't possibly afford them. The price of any leveraged asset is ultimately directly proportional to the availability of credit used to finance it. The structured finance industry hasn't been completely dismantled after the financial crisis but it will never be the same. It will likely take another three generations of bankers and politicians to devise "new" methods of financing that would allow us to re-create the mass delusion that real estate prices can't decline. While we have reached a bottom in housing in terms of units, stable price appreciation seems to be taking hold only now, more than six years after the bubble burst.

All of these busted myths led many of us to wonder who we can turn to in the future when the academic basis for our industry has been turned completely upside down. There are no easy answers for this but I suspect that the answers that do exist lie not in fancy academic journals and textbooks, but in the more fundamental concepts of fiduciary responsibility, knowing one's customer, and common sense.

For the skeptic and the true believer alike, many of the quantitative building blocks of modern finance that led many financial engineers to believe in their almost godlike ability to slice and dice risk came crashing down with the failure of Lehman Brothers in September 2008. I realized then as a middle-aged man who owned an apartment in Manhattan, a brokerage firm, and common stocks that despite my best efforts to be financially conservative, my life was filled with financial risks both seen and unseen. There's nothing like a global financial crisis (and the red brackets on your statements that accompany it) to make you lie awake at night and think about what you might have missed in all those years of formal education.

I was fortunate enough to attend great schools and I've wondered more times than I care to admit in the last few years whether I learned a damn thing in Philadelphia; I've also wondered at times whether it was my own lack of interest in my studies or the "system" that left me feeling so intellectually hopeless as the markets melted down. Perhaps a testament to rationalization, I've come to the conclusion that the broader, more liberal arts–oriented courses I took at Georgetown did far more to help me adapt to what was deemed "economically unprecedented" than the more technical lessons I learned in business school. Not once since the financial crisis began have I felt compelled to develop more complex mathematical models to help me discern what is happening. This is due at least in part to an almost immediate revelation that it was these same models that sowed the seeds of the financial collapse in the first place. The financial crisis didn't prompt me to do more mathematics; it encouraged me to read quite a bit more history. Formerly disgraced financier-cum-philanthropist and perhaps Wharton's most famous (or infamous) graduate, Michael Milken, commented: "Perhaps more discussion of actual human beings might prevent some of its graduates from committing some of the most basic human mistakes first categorized by the Greeks two thousand years ago."

This isn't to say that business school has no place in one's education as a businessman, but simply that the ratio of what was taught to me about systems, processes, theories, and mathematics to what was taught to me about real people was probably a thousand to one. In fact, it is not an exaggeration to say that a graduate from a top business school would never have been introduced to the likes of J. P. Morgan, Andrew Carnegie, Cornelius Vanderbilt, Jay Gould, or John Rockefeller. Perhaps more shocking, a business school graduate is also unlikely to have been taught all that much about the history and theory of the corporation and its relationship and responsibility to its shareholders, employees, local community, or board of directors.

There is no denying that math and science are critical to America's economic future. One can't help wondering, however, whether too many of our math and science students are using their studies to become financial engineers rather than real engineers who go on to develop innovations that make businesses more productive, improve standards of living and provide the basis of the accumulation of wealth and capital that go along with them.

Finance is an important discipline and Wall Street provides an invaluable service to society, breathing life into the dreams that only capitalism can inspire. But a greater recognition that finance is at its heart a social science—with all the uncertainty that marks human interactions—would no doubt make would-be financiers more humble, less dangerous, and, by extension, more useful. A greater emphasis on economic history could arm students with a basic humanity that could remind them that outside of the laws of science two hundred thousand years of recorded human history demonstrate that there are few certainties in life and that the basic human emotions of pride, fear, and greed can turn the seemingly impossible into a stark reality very quickly. My ninth-grade social studies teacher (even then I guess it was considered outré to call it history) would be happy to know that I remember the first thing she wrote on the blackboard thirty years ago: "Those who do not know their past are condemned to repeat it. Santayana." She would, however, be sad to learn that after all these years I still have no earthly idea who Santayana was or why he was important.

As it says in Ecclesiastes, there is nothing new under the sun, which helps me understand that while the names may change, human beings are in many ways immutable in their arrogance and self-deception. I finally did start to understand what Erasmus was getting at in his *Praise of Folly*, which mocked mathematicians and scientists for their intellectual arrogance:

The common people are especially disdained when they bring out their triangles, quadrangles, circles, and mathematical figures of the like. They place one on top of the other and arrange them into a maze. Then they deploy some letters precisely, as if in a battle formation, and finally they reverse them. And all of this is done only to confuse those who are ignorant of their field. These scientists do not like those who predict the future from the stars, and promise even more fantastic miracles. And these fortunate men find people who believe them.

Of course, these insights were developed only after I had made all the same mistakes MBA students make upon graduation. When I left business school, nothing could have been more important to me than starting my career on Wall Street anew. At twenty-seven, taking the time to learn about things like the history of my business felt akin to cutting years off of my professional life.

Ultimately I made the same mistake everyone else made. I went for the bucks and the prestige. I didn't take time to consider whether my job on a foreign exchange sales desk would make me happy or be well suited to whatever modest talents I possessed. It promised enough cachet that I was satisfied and didn't have to spend much time explaining to my parents what I was going to be doing. It sounded prestigious enough to impress my friends and people I met at cocktail parties. It filled my brain with visions of having coffee with central bankers in Berne while debating the weighty issues facing the world of international finance, and maybe even a few of those chance encounters with exotic women.

FIND THE HUMANITY:

Core Curricula of America's Elite Business Schools

Wharton

Fall and Spring Core
Accounting
Corporate Finance
Macroeconomics Ethics and Responsibility
Management of People at Work
Competitive Strategy
Global Strategic Management

Marketing Management
Operations Management
Statistical Analysis
Management Communication

Harvard

Finance
Financial Reporting and Control
Leadership and Organizational Behavior
Marketing
Technology and Operations Management

Business, Government, and the International Economy
Strategy
The Entrepreneurial Manager
Leadership and Corporate Accountability

5

BIG HAT, NO CATTLE

One night Billy convinced me, as a foreign exchange sales trader straight out of business school, to have drinks with one of the rising stars at a macro hedge fund rapidly becoming one of the sell side's biggest customers. Scott was a buy-side trader who handled FX and seemed far less interested in talking about the markets than in impressing us with his newfound status and his knowledge of expensive automobiles, velvet-rope clubs in the Village, and his favorite vacation spots.

"You're crazy. St. Bart's is the best place on earth."

"I don't know. If the weather's good, I kind of like Bermuda—" I offered, never having been to St. Bart's myself.

"You see that girl over there. If she had better hair and lost weight, she'd be a knockout. If you want to go cheap, spend six or seven hundred dollars a night, and hang out with people like her from Summit, Bermuda's the place. If you want to go for the big time, live in luxury, and have hot French chicks hit on you even when you're with your wife, then it's St. Bart's or it's nothing."

On the outside, I smiled and nodded in agreement and said he was probably right. The customer is always right, of course. But on the inside, my mind started to wander and I began to silently ask myself, "Who the fuck talks like this? What kind of cosmic accident has allowed so many of us, as mediocrities, to be so well paid?" The chances of a "hot French chick" hitting on Scott, ever, were about as high as Jessica Alba randomly seeking me out to start a new life at a beachside resort in Brazil. I lamped him for a guy who was never good at sports, earned a reputation in his public high school in Bergen County as an overachieving kiss ass, and barely got out of there alive. It didn't matter that Billy and I had just met him and that we were buying the drinks. He was another big hat, no cattle hedge fund guy born on third base who had convinced himself he'd hit a triple. For the first time in his life, he could picture himself as a romantic character. As his "coverage" as trader and sales trader respectively, Billy and I could do nothing but agree.

In spite of having worked on Wall Street for four years before business school, I was still trying to reconcile what I really wanted to do on the Street with what I thought others would find most impressive. For whatever reason—ego and pride mostly—I convinced myself that I wanted to be a trader. It seemed to offer a good combination of money, prestige, excitement, and arrested development that would be appealing to many guys in their twenties. During an internship at Merrill Lynch between my first and second years at Wharton, I had managed to piss off nearly everyone at the company with my naked ambition, no easy feat at a firm with forty thousand people. The guys who traded corporate bonds largely saw me, I was to find out, as a little too eager to make my way on Wall Street. Merrill was a deeply political place where quiet ambition was appreciated, and my approach was, correctly as I can see now, despised and controversial. Still consumed with the idea that success on the Street required a fire in the belly, that summer I often visited the relative value desk run by Anshu Jain (now the co-CEO of Deutsche Bank) at 5:30 a.m. on the

football field–sized trading floor on 7 before my regularly scheduled rotation at any of the firm's other sales and trading departments, including my future home, foreign exchange. Despite the
fact I was not offered a permanent job to start after I graduated
with an MBA, I didn't give up. I somehow managed to convince
the head of the foreign exchange desk to take me on the following July.

In reality, I shared a half desk and a Bloomberg Terminal (Merrill then owned 30 percent of the company) with a co-worker. I
found myself watching the five-minute moving average versus the
ten-minute moving average of Dollar-Mark and quickly realized
that there are few financial instruments where fundamental analysis can kill you faster than in foreign exchange. Trading FX was
largely dependent on technical analysis: detailed examinations of
charts and price patterns were all that really mattered for those
trading the spot market. In these markets, having good judgment
isn't enough and the ability to assess changes in the markets *quickly*
is critical. Reading the paper and developing a well-reasoned thesis about the direction of the economy was actually an occupational hazard because you'd have a tendency to think more than
you should, missing opportunities for profit, and, more important, to avoid losses at the right time. This was ultimately my
problem and why I was ill equipped for the job. The only customers I was able to convince to do business with me were small re-
gional Italian banks that appreciated the opportunity to talk about
Jenny McCarthy in Italian to some guy in New York. It was hard
to build a career in FX trading dollar-lira at $500,000 a clip, let
me tell you. It didn't take me long to wonder whether pursuing
my MBA was a total waste of time and money. I had depleted my
savings, was $60,000 in debt, and had missed three years of a bull
market to get a job that I wasn't particularly interested in or good
at. In the dog-eat-dog atmosphere of Merrill Lynch, swiping my

ID card through the security turnstiles that guarded entry to the firm required a leap of technological faith that was rivaled only by my visits to the ATM machine in college. Like Diogenes, I believed I had lost my way and was looking for an honest man. Mercifully, I found one in an old colleague, my friend Alan Goldman.

One night, while I was crying in my beer about my predicament at a bar in Hoboken, he told me simply that I was looking for fulfillment on Wall Street in the wrong places.

"A trading desk is no place for you," he said. "You're not tough enough. You like to write, you love macro, and you like being in front of customers. You really ought to be a strategist."

Up until that point, I had viewed strategists as a rarefied species. People like Elaine Garzarelli and Lee Cooperman were legends. Still, Alan told me, you had to start somewhere. It would be another example where others saw things about my life more clearly than I did. It may sound melodramatic but that one conversation made all the difference in my career, for it was at that point that I truly realized what I wanted to do. At important stages of my short tenure on Wall Street until then, my insecurities led me to choose jobs with the express purpose of impressing other people rather than doing something that I might actually like and—more important from the standpoint of an employer—that I might be good at. In the most public way possible, I was trying to get 21 at the blackjack table, when the object of the game was to beat the dealer. Focusing on status rather than achievement is a mistake that will forever be made by young people on Wall Street. Some never grow out of it. My best friend, Jay, told me once about a portfolio manager at the legendary firm Tiger who would at times question how "smart" its founder Julian Robertson really was. Jay's simple free-market analysis always expresses a "beat-the-dealer" spirit:

"In the money management business," he said, "there's only one objective measure of intelligence and that's money. By that standard Julian is one of the smartest guys that ever set foot on Wall Street. Period."

I was also beginning to get smarter. I realized how many people on Wall Street confused their ability to project status with actual achievement. They painted the tape with their own lives, making a series of life decisions and transactions designed to manipulate other people's perceptions of their personal net worth rather than making a real attempt to accomplish anything of substance. It starts with using car services for personal use (the most pervasive abuse of any Wall Street firm's expense accounts), escalates into ordering the seafood tower at Smith and Wollensky's, morphs into beach houses bought with 10 percent down, and too often culminates with trophy wives who have the same hang-ups and annoying habits as the original article.

All of this would become more apparent after I started my own firm and began to interview salesmen and sales traders extensively. On Wall Street, as in other places of business, especially at the large investment banks known as bulge brackets, for every dollar of revenue that comes through the door, eight hands will be raised to claim credit for it. The average Wall Street guy completely overestimates his value to the firm's business and underestimates the value of the opportunity he's been given by dint of the firm he works for. This is best exemplified by the "I know a guy" syndrome. The interview process with experienced institutional salesmen involves determining just how much of the revenue he's generated has been due to his efforts rather than those of the firm.

"How's your relationship with Acme Capital Partners?"

"Couldn't be better. The head trader, Joe, and I play in his member/guest every year and I stay at his house. I think I can also get you into ABC. *I know a guy* over there really well."

Occasionally these claims are true, but more often than not

they are overestimates or complete fabrications. Most of the time this isn't due to a desire to deceive. It's simply due to the fact that no one really knows how to value a salesman's efforts at a large bulge bracket firm that offers everything from research to trade execution to margin lending to a variety of other services that are impossible to disaggregate. One of the old saws about the difficulty of valuing brokerage firms is that "the assets go up and down the elevators every day." There are those who have changed this bon mot to "the assholes go up and down the elevators every day" but the sentiment is still the same. The only real assets of a brokerage firm are the people who work there and, unlike other industries, the talent can walk across the street and get another job without the drama of looking for a new home or pulling their kids out of school.

That people tend to overestimate their skills is nothing new. Psychologists have noted that more than 75 percent of any group of people surveyed will describe themselves as above-average drivers. On Wall Street these tendencies tend to be exaggerated mainly because of the money. A number of "real" companies found this out the hard way when the temptation of outsized Wall Street earnings proved too alluring to pass up. When the investment banking business was hot in the 1980s, it was fashionable for large industrial companies to try to get in on the action by buying brokerage firms. Xerox bought Furman Selz and, most famously, General Electric bought Kidder, Peabody. To say that these acquisitions turned out to be disasters would be an understatement. Although GE wound up eventually making money on its purchase of Kidder in 1987, the amount of distracted time, stress, and negative impact on the parent firm's culture led Jack Welch to conclude that it was one of the worst deals he ever made in a stellar business career. The differences between the culture of an industrial company and a Wall Street firm became apparent almost immediately.

In his book *Jack: Straight from the Gut,* Welch summed up almost perfectly how different Wall Street firms are from normal businesses:

> Frankly, the bonus numbers knocked most of us off our pins when we saw them. At the time, GE's total bonus pool was just under $100 million a year for a company making $4 billion in profit. Kidder's bonus pool was actually higher— at $140 million—for a company that was earning only one-twentieth of our income. Si [Cathcart, Kidder's newly installed CEO] remembers that on the day Kidder employees got their bonus checks, the place would clear out in an hour. "You could shoot a cannon off without hitting anyone," he told me. Most of them lived a lifestyle dependent on those annual bonuses. It was a different world from what Si or I knew . . . The attitudes were symbolic of the problems of an entitlement culture where every player overvalued themselves. Where God parachutes us is a matter of luck. Nowhere is that more true than Wall Street. There are more mediocre people making more money on Wall Street than any other place on earth.*

Warren Buffett has also noted the misplaced confidences of people on Wall Street and the unjustified reverence people from "flyover country," who run more prosaic businesses, pay them. Too often, the Wall Street punk in a Brioni suit doesn't realize that the tool and die business guy from Fargo sitting across from him wearing polyester could buy and sell him ten times over. Oversized egos and attitudes of entitlement were further exacerbated when Wall Street became televised, its major protagonists going from bit players to celebrities in a matter of three short years.

---

* Jack Welch with John A. Byrne, *Jack—Straight from the Gut,* New York: Business Plus, 2001, 221.

Dealing with a hypercompetitive group of people who measure life's score with dollars and cents leads to often-ridiculous attempts to satisfy the ugly twin sisters of pride and vanity. When I first got out of school, my buddy Scott worked for the aforementioned Kidder, Peabody, still among the top ten, but hardly a top-tier player in investment banking. Kidder maintained a real and almost defiant inferiority complex vis-à-vis the majors like Goldman Sachs, Morgan Stanley, and Salomon Brothers. As a young vice-president on the real estate deal team, Scott, and Kidder, Peabody, through some quirk of luck, found themselves as the lead manager on a deal with Goldman. (One must remember that a firm's placement on the "tombstone" announcing the sale of securities is of primary importance for calendar managers.) As the lead, Kidder had the privilege of having all the other investment banks visit their offices for meetings. Since this rarely happened, everybody was a little nervous and wanted to show the guys from Goldman that they were really peers, whatever perceived differences in reputation being merely a function of hype. Kidder ordered an expensive spread of sushi and prepared the firm's boardroom for their guests. They wore their best duds—including suspenders with yellow power ties—and gave the receptionist on the floor very specific instructions how to treat their rivals. The appointed hour came and Scott and his colleagues in the conference room waited eagerly for their competitors. They were ready to show those self-important assholes from Goldman just how good they were. In walked Kidder's receptionist, trailed by the very earnest and smug bankers from Goldman. As if rehearsing her lines, the receptionist made a very dramatic introduction and, outstretching her arm, said:

"Gentlemen, let me introduce your guests from *Golden Slacks*."

It was one of those rare moments that is so embarrassing and comical no one could utter even the smallest of laughs. Kidder's deal team was defeated before the meeting even started, and the guys from Goldman were allowed to continue to feel smug at an away game.

Wall Street self-importance can best be exemplified by the semifictional character of Charlie Vitellone, an institutional salesman who became addicted to the good life. An All-American lacrosse player from Virginia, he had no trouble getting a job on a trading desk after graduation. His dad was an engineer at Grumman, his mother a housewife, and they were solidly in the middle class. He knew nothing of the good life until he came to Wall Street. Soon he was living *la dolce vita*, having a variety of girlfriends, going to Vail with clients in the winter, and the Hamptons with his buddies in the summer. He caught a wave in the eighties and nineties and found himself preposterously rich by the time he was forty, married, with kids in private school, a boat, and two club memberships. The twenty extra pounds he put on since his college days were well concealed by Turnbull and Asser shirts and Vineyard Vines ties. He got accustomed to the money and never really paused to consider what would happen if the music stopped. Having close to eight figures in company stock, he simply assumed he never had to worry about money again.

He never sold a share. Things started to get a little tougher after the Internet bubble burst and his once seven-figure salary fell to about half that. He didn't know how it happened but he was suddenly trapped at $500,000 a year. Things got worse after the financial crisis when his company stock fell by 80 percent. He'd given his life to the company and while he'd made no enemies he hadn't developed more than a handful of true friendships with his customers. At that point he really didn't have friends as much as he had interests. The good news is that his firm wouldn't let him go because he does too much business with obscure accounts and knows too much about where the bodies are buried to ever get fired. And yet, still at a level of compensation that would make most people who lived far away from the canyons of Wall Street weep with envy, he sometimes felt sorry for himself.

He had dreams of moving to a part of the country where his savings would render him rich again. But his kids are in New York and he can't bear to leave them with his now-estranged wife. His father passed away but his mother lives in a retirement home in Glen Cove. And so he's resigned himself to the fact that he's in for the grind and tries to forget about all the money he pissed away trying to impress other people with his own life. Wealth, especially paper wealth, should never be taken for granted.

At twenty-eight, I finally became less interested in style points and more interested in real points. The day after the epiphany I received from a saint named Alan Goldman at a bar in Hoboken, I called my old boss Ed Hyman and pitched the idea of using my education and my new perspective to be a strategist for ISI. Given my lack of experience, this was ridiculous. But I believed Ed could sense that I had found and was excited about a new path. I wasn't qualified enough at that point to hold such a job at a firm known to be the best macroeconomic provider on Wall Street, but he wondered whether I might be interested in running another research product for the firm that might lead to my ultimate professional aspiration of being a market prognosticator.

The project involved creating a number of industry surveys and, like everyone else I graduated with from business school, I had to rely on simple old-fashioned moxie rather than any formal education. Simply put, I had to call the treasurer's office at a variety of public companies once a week and ask them, on a scale of 1 to 5, how their revenues were tracking. A 3 was on-plan. We would then aggregate the numbers to protect the identities of the individual companies and interpolate our findings on a 0 to 100 scale. As one might imagine, many executives didn't really cotton to the idea of telling a complete stranger about their business, but enough did to make it work. Mercifully, our firm's economic work soon became a vital part of the way these executives thought about their own firms. Not doing any company-specific research, it also became apparent that we would never betray the confidences of the companies themselves. The research project, rather uncreatively named the Company Survey Report, was an immediate hit with clients. It was simple to understand, it was unique, and it allowed them to get real-time economic information at a time when the money management business was getting more competitive. All the while, I wrote investment essays once a month to pave the way to what I saw as my eventual career as a strategist. The irony is that while the survey product wasn't fun to do (who wants to make a couple of hundred calls asking the same question week after week?), it was useful. Strategy work, on the other hand, was enormously fun to do, although there were times when you wondered whether it was useful at all. As John Kenneth Galbraith once remarked, "There are two types of economists—those that don't know and those that don't know they don't know."

But I learned something else in the process of making those never-ending phone calls that served me well later on: it's entirely possible (even likely) that a Wall Street strategist or economist can spend his entire career pontificating about the economy and the markets without ever talking to anyone who's ever gotten their hands dirty building a real business. Spend a day calling eight trucking companies or fifty auto dealers or six airlines and you start to realize that there are plenty of Wall Street economists, and public policy makers for that matter, who are completely and utterly full of it. It was to Ed Hyman's credit that he realized the importance of the company surveys, not only for commercial purposes but to inform his own research. Other more academic economists on the Street sometimes laughed at the project, calling it pop economics. It was a funny thing, though: the institutional investors who were our clients never dismissed the project's findings. They just kept voting Ed the number one economist on Wall Street.

Things didn't become magically easier once I realized that the secret was to ignore other people's successes, real or alleged, and to focus on my goals alone. I had to take more than my fair share of hits in the backfield to advance my career from that point forward, but I had found my road less traveled and it made all the difference.

6

THE CUSTOMER MAN'S
TWO-FRONT WAR

his may strike some as an odd chapter, perhaps even a
risky one. Anyone who has made it this far has probably
already realized that mine is a story of arrested development and some would say anachronistic views of the business. But
integral to my story—and perhaps to the story of any married or
once-married man on Wall Street—is the two-front war: the central tension between our responsibilities to our families at home
and our families at work, our own little band of brothers. And
central to our complicated dealings with women are the relatively
new and almost-constant attempts to square the roles our mothers
played—even if they worked outside the home holding down a
job—with roles the women in our lives play today. In the space of
a generation, it seems all the rules have changed. Remaining single would have eased the burden that accompanied my ambition
but it would have been a waste. How else would I experience the
greater truths of life that really only evidence themselves with
the arrival of children and the need to be, for the first time,
truly selfless.

Everyone knows that men tend to be obsessed with women.

And Wall Street, due to the perpetual adolescence the industry can nurture, is probably home to more skirt chasers than any other business, with the possible exception of politics. Although I spent virtually every waking hour of my single life chasing women before I married one, I can't say that I understand them any better now than when they first became the objects of my desire. The differences between men and women are legion but if there is one difference I've noticed between how the genders treat their careers and their ambitions it is simply this: a man looks at the least competent person doing the job he covets and assumes, almost always correctly, that he could do no worse. Many women, for some reason, look at the most successful person in the same situation and assume, often incorrectly, that they could do no better. Ultimately, this can be attributed to an overconfidence in the average male and a lack of confidence and a hesitancy to "lean in" in the average woman. The funny thing is that this is, in many ways, why men chase women. Women's insecurities tend to make them eager to please and often make them more empathetic to those who struggle. Unfortunately, it also tends to lead to overthinking, overanalyzing, and a perverse need to make the perfect the enemy of the good. Is this a gross generalization that reflects an outdated view of the world and of women? Probably. Almost definitely. But any honest and sentient being who has worked in an office knows that there are obvious differences between the sexes that evidence themselves every day and in every way, most often during times of stress.

Again, this Cro-Magnon view of the fairer sex derives from something so primal it must have been a part of my upbringing. As noted above, my mom is a very well-educated woman who has never lived a life of wealth and privilege, having grown up in an almost stereotypical Italian immigrant household in the Gravesend section of Brooklyn. She never knew much about wealth or privilege, or even the appearance of wealth and privilege, and is still amazed, despite a life of hard work and savings, at the cost of nearly everything and the willingness of people to pay more than what she believes is fair for just about everything. This is clearly a function of having been born during the Depression and the fact that for most of her life easy access to credit, and thus the ability to even fake affluence, was impossible. To her, private clubs and summer homes and all the other trappings of the well-to-do remain impractical uses of money. So I am often intrigued by her reactions to a life I've started to take for granted. This is most apparent during Christmastime, when I put my mom up at the New York Athletic Club on Central Park South, the only time of the year she spends time with me in what has become my hometown. Although it is hardly among New York City's most elite private clubs, the NYAC was established in 1868 by Henry Buermeyer, John Babcock, and William Curtis. Its members have won more than 230 Olympic medals since its founding. While the club was, tragically, at one time restricted to wealthy white Christian men (New York Mayor Robert F. Wagner resigned in 1962 in protest), it has since become much more cosmopolitan. I had never set foot in a private club of any kind until I applied for NYAC membership at the urging of a client when I was twenty-four. It is a wonderful place staffed by kind people and it retains an old-world charm reminiscent of New York at the turn of the twentieth century, so it would be easy to see how the uninitiated might find it intimidating. One Christmas Day when we were taking the elevator down from the dining room on the eleventh floor, my mom and I were joined by three young couples, each leaner, blonder, richer, and more WASPishly angular in facial features than the next. Their conversations were clipped and the women seemed oddly tense, the men somehow intimidated.

As we walked out of the building, my mom asked, innocently,

"Are all the women in Manhattan like that?" (While she grew up less than fifteen miles away, Manhattan still remains a "ritzy" foreign land to her.)

"Like what, Ma?"

"They seem so . . . I don't know . . . so brittle."

This was yet another example of how others see things about our lives that we are too close to notice. She was right. Many high achieving men and women in New York *are* brittle—so hard, so full of high expectations of their lives and their families—it seems even the slightest vibration in the rarefied air surrounding them could shatter them into a million tiny pieces. I immediately remembered Hemingway's line from "The Short Happy Life of Francis Macomber," a story that at its core is about courage, especially for men caught in the glare when under pressure from privileged women: "They are, he thought, the hardest in the world; the hardest, the cruelest, the most predatory and the most attractive and their men have softened or gone to pieces nervously as they have hardened. Or is it that they pick men they can handle?"

Perhaps it was a function of the fact that my family remained solidly in the middle class with no great ambitions to be upwardly mobile, but my mom and my aunts could never have been described as brittle. When I was a kid my parents argued over just about everything—money, meals, real or imagined flirtations, politics. You name it. But I know that they never, not once, fought about the division of labor around the house. My mom never complained that my dad wasn't doing his fair share of the housework or spending enough time looking after my care and welfare. Of course they grew up in a different era in which women were expected to deal with the things inside the house and the men were responsible for the things outside of it. My mom was the third child of eight, born to a housewife and a longshoreman on the Manhattan dockyards, my grandfather Fiore. Her mother died tragically of rheumatic fever when my mom was only thirteen, forcing her and her sisters to become surrogate mothers to the five younger children, the youngest of whom, my uncle Rich, was two when my grandmother passed away in 1949. My mom and my aunts Elsie and Marilyn had to cook, clean, change diapers, and all the rest. As the oldest sister, my aunt Elsie was forced to leave high school and married my uncle Lou as soon as he got out of the service. The two remaining sisters in the house had to balance their own education and development with the welfare of the younger children. Despite it all, my mom became quite a modern woman. She graduated from Brooklyn College, where she was the editor of the college newspaper, and eventually enrolled in the graduate school of journalism at Columbia. She dropped out when she met and married my dad and never lamented the fact that she became a teacher rather than a famous journalist as some of her classmates did. Given that background, it isn't all that surprising that my father and I immediately left the table after eating dinner to watch sports or play Ping-Pong or whatever. The kitchen was my mom's responsibility. She dutifully prepared the meals and, quietly and without protest, cleaned up afterward. There's nothing noble about this. It was just the way it was.

There is no doubt that some modern women would see this as a form of indentured servitude and perhaps it was. But there was no other choice when my mom was at home in Brooklyn and she expected little else when she started her own family. Trust me. This is not a woman who would suffer silently if she had any other problems with my father. My mother worked just as hard as my father as a teacher. She never felt any need, nor did my dad, to keep up with the Joneses. They were products of an era in which one was simply happy to have a job with health benefits. Questions of personal fulfillment—of finding oneself—were so fanciful to them as to be hardly considered.

Things have been different, to put it mildly, since I started my own family. My wife is truly one of the great ones, and I mean it. She doesn't care about money and is shy and unpretentious. Our challenges as a family arose after my son was born and the modern realities of working women became clear. Let's face it, most men are, at best, unenthusiastic, and at worst, useless, when helping out around the home regardless of the challenges their wives might face at work. Naturally our celebrity-based culture doesn't help matters. A typical gossip rag today will, with a straight face, lionize men who go through women like tissue paper and provide in-depth "you can have it all" type features on an over-the-hill starlet, married four times, who regales readers about her ability to balance both life and work from her ten-thousand-square-foot mansion in Malibu, the messy details of life outsourced to domestic help, her salary ten million a picture. It is even more mystifying to me why wealthy men believe they can shirk their responsibilities as fathers and husbands in favor of their business careers without realizing that it will eventually weigh heavily on their souls. Ultimately, men will be judged more by the way they treat their families than by any other achievement.

At the time we married, my wife, Bev, had a good job in corporate communications at a major bond insurer in Manhattan. Things were going well enough for us financially that there was no need for her to go back to work after my son, Dominic, was born. I'm not quite sure, to this day, if she even wanted to go back to work. But she insisted, committed to not having a clichéd Wall Street family life. I wasn't, to be honest, very helpful at home and I regret it. I was traveling close to a hundred days a year back then and wasn't exactly the type that would wear a BabyBjörn. I still drank with the boys and fought what I perceived to be unfair expectations of a husband and father who had a job that required total commitment. Combine this with the fact that my son was, from day one, a natural but incredibly lovable *rompicoglioni* and it isn't hard to imagine why we were miserable a good part of the time those first five years—exhausted and irritable and unhappy.

Eventually my wife probably came to the conclusion that someone needed to take up the slack around the home and it was unlikely to be me. Mercifully, it turned out to be a blessing for us as a family. Immediately everyone, perhaps most especially my wife, was happier. Realizing I was in part responsible for her decision to give up her job and feeling somewhat guilty about it, I tried to help out a little more around the house. Another blessed result was the birth of a second child, my daughter, Marie. God apparently decided that we suffered enough with the vicissitudes of my son's eating and sleeping habits, and gave us an easy child.

This isn't necessarily particular to Wall Street, of course, although both the financial industry and the credit machine on which it was allowed to grow have distributed high-class problems to a variety of people. Families who were once content can now, because one can feel trapped at $350,000 a year in New York, never really feel completely content again. Money is the greatest of all false prophets. Now in my midforties, I see them lining the borders of lacrosse fields in Greenwich and Bronxville and on the Upper East Side, women, who, in many cases, have absurdly unrealistic expectations of married life—especially to a Wall Street guy who has to commute. Many find that their money can't isolate them from pain, solitude, boredom, aggravation, and the thousands of other annoyances to which human flesh is heir. They find that the lady filling their prescriptions behind the counter at Duane Reade, possessed by a certain aggressive ennui that comes with a dead-end job, couldn't possibly care less that her husband is a managing director in M&A at Lazard. The ladies behind the counter care even less that her father was an ophthalmologist in

Oceanside. Even if one is affluent enough to be able to afford to hire cutouts to deal with life's difficulties, one is likely to find that money can only get you so far.

The result is often a sense of leading a life unfulfilled and haunted by near-constant comparisons with other Wall Street families that are similarly built on misperceptions of perfection. The contest is unwinnable because it isn't real and it comes from within. The best arbiters of character for these parents are often their kids. Because they don't understand the larger world around them and tend to assume that most people live almost exactly like they do. They understand what's truly important, in some ways more than their parents do. The only thing kids really crave is the time and encouragement of their parents. For many Wall Street kids, the country clubs and the fancy vacations aren't special in any way. It's expected.

More than a few men have sought to relieve the pressure to create the storybook lives their wives seek in the company of other women. This "solution" almost always reveals itself to be a cruel and ironic joke (the women they choose have the same unrealistic expectations) and can tragically end in divorce. In the movie *Moonstruck*, Olympia Dukakis spends a considerable amount of time trying to figure out why her husband was straying. The movie's almost constant refrain was a simple question: "Why do men chase women?" She finally gets her answer from an unlikely source, a suitor her daughter doesn't love. Played by Danny Aiello, the suitor's reply was simple: "Because they fear death." One of the funny things about a lot of men is that they spend all of their time thinking about women until they're actually with one. Then they think about golf, ESPN, other women, money, the money needed to attract other women, mob movies. You name it. For most men, attaining a relationship with a woman is a lot more fun than the relationship itself.

Mercifully, quite a few men make some sort of peace with the two-front war of keeping both their family at work and their family at home happy. While the married man in his twenties thinks himself invincible and will sometimes seek out trouble, the man in his forties, if he is to survive without going crazy, understands that trouble will sometimes find him. For a man with a wife and kids and especially one who has seen his net worth decline in the past few years, such chances just aren't worth the risk. His struggles have oddly made him appreciate his family a bit more and made him realize that a lot of his "friends" were really just friends as long as he was scoring touchdowns. Temptation still exists and there are vagaries of life that can put even the most honorable man in no-win situations when trying to square the responsibilities of a career and a family. My buddy Tommy, for example, is an institutional salesman at a midtier investment bank in Boston. His wife used to work in the business and knows Tommy once had a relationship, before they were married, with a now aging sexpot, "Tess," who's a portfolio manager at his largest account. Predictably, Tommy's wife hates her. But it's a big company with plenty of portfolio managers and they've remained friends and all is right with the world. That was until his firm's Christmas party for clients two years ago. There were about a hundred people there all in all, and a number of the people he covered at his largest account were in attendance, including its chief investment officer and, naturally, his former flame. Tommy flitted around from client to client, took it easy on the sauce, and started to look forward to the sleep of the just. What he didn't notice was that Tess was getting blind drunk. That was until the head guy at an account representing about a third of Tommy's book sidled up to him toward the end of the evening.

"Tommy, you've been friends with Tess for a long time, right?"

"Uh, yeah, sure," he said hesitating, now worried.

"Well, she's starting to make a complete ass of herself and I'd like someone to take her home before it really gets embarrassing. You live in Cohasset and she's in Hingham. Would you mind making sure she gets home all right?"

No good choices here. He can't say no to his largest client and he would rather avoid—as a man with some modicum of pride— telling him that his wife wouldn't approve. Still, he worries for two reasons—the temptation—and, even if he were able to resist it, the fear that his wife would never believe him if she found out he took her home without incident. But this shop puts bread on the table and really there is no choice.

"Sure, Bill," Tommy responds. "I'll take care of it."

He says his good-byes and somehow manages to pour Tess into his leased BMW 5 Series and just starts to pray that he's able to get home without a guilty conscience. But Tess is a mess. She takes off her shoes and her coat, blasts Classic Vinyl, won't shut up, begins to reminisce, and starts to play with his tie. Tommy soldiers on and despite her entreaties to stay, he gets her into her house without any moral consequences. Crisis averted—largest client happy, old girlfriend safe, and no guilt.

The next evening was a Friday, when he and his wife typically leave the kids with a babysitter and go out to dinner or a movie. But this was a special occasion—his wife's birthday. They were dressed elegantly. She asked a few questions about the party the night before, but Tommy got home early and in good shape and so she avoided the subject of Tess altogether. At a certain point she wants to show him something in *Cape Cod* magazine in a seat pocket in the back of the car. She unfastens her seatbelt and climbs halfway into the back to find the article. As she does this, a five-inch high-heeled shoe rolls out from under her seat. Tommy starts to sweat. In a flash, his mind races from visions of dramatic fights with his wife to difficult conversations with the kids to divorce court. Shame. Poverty. Public golf courses. Flying coach. Oh, the humanity. Stopped at a red light, he lowers his window, reaches for the smoking gun, and, in one swift move, heaves the incriminating evidence across three lanes of traffic. His wife never stops talking, finds the magazine in question, and finally sits back comfortably in her seat. Tommy's heart rate just went from 80 to 170 and is now starting to decline gradually, the beads of sweat from his forehead cooling as he shuts off the heat. About ten minutes later they arrive at the fancy French restaurant that has been home of many a happy occasion for the couple. He gets out of the car and starts walking toward the entrance. After about twenty feet, he notices his wife is still in the car and again starts to fear the worst.

"What's the matter honey, are you OK?"

"No!" she says frustrated. "For some reason I can't find my left shoe. I took them off when I got in the car and somehow I lost one."

At this point, Tommy doesn't know whether to laugh hysterically or to start to cry. No good deed, as they say, goes unpunished.

Having explained the male point of view, I guess it's only fair that I try to make sense of the difficulties of women trying to make their way on Wall Street. There is little question that women have made great strides in the financial services industry over the years. They've come a long way from the time it was seen as almost blasphemous that a woman named Muriel Siebert bought a seat on the NYSE in 1967. Of the first ten men she asked to sponsor her application for membership, nine refused. The big board finally relented and she would remain the only woman admitted to membership for almost a decade.

The progress has been most impressive in every aspect of modern finance—investment banking, research, trading, money management—except the one with which I am most familiar: institutional sales. There have been and continue to be countless examples of famous and successful female Wall Street professionals—Virginia Woodhull and Tennessee Claflin, who opened up the first female-owned brokerage firm on Wall Street; Hetty Green, who became so rich as an investor that she loaned New York City $1 million in 1898; Elaine Garzarelli, who "called" the crash in 1987; Abby Joseph Cohen, Goldman's legendary investment strategist; and, in the realm of financial journalism, my friend and fellow *paisà*, Maria Bartiromo, who, aside from being the face of the growth in investment media, was the first reporter to broadcast live from the floor of the New York Stock Exchange.

My favorite story of a successful woman on Wall Street, however, belongs to Isabel Benham, perhaps the most acclaimed sell-side analyst, man or woman, ever. Born in Upstate New York in 1909, Benham started her career on Wall Street after graduating from Bryn Mawr in economics at the depths of the Great Depression in 1934. In 1964, after following the railroad industry for nearly thirty years with famed brokerage firm R. W. Pressprich and Co., she became the firm's first female partner in its fifty-five-year history. She took the road less traveled, never married or had children, and fought her way onto Wall Street only after taking a six-month bond sales course underwritten by her father. She eventually left Pressprich with its managing partner, Charlie Bergmann, to build a railroad department at Shearson Hammill and Co., and eventually became president of the firm Printon, Kane Research before retiring in 1991. When asked in a *Forbes* magazine profile in 1985 whether she had to be one of the boys to succeed on Wall Street, she said, "In my day, we wore white gloves and hats. Some women seem to think they can get ahead, aside from being smart, by being able to swear, drink and tell dirty stories with the boys. You didn't play around with the boys in 1934. And it's not necessary today, in my opinion. I have worked with a lot of men and never once have they sworn in front of me in meetings." She lived to be 103, passing away just this past year in Manhattan.

As the proprietor of my own firm now, I push my salesmen to do as much traveling and entertaining as possible, not as an expectation of quid pro quo, but rather as an attempt by a small firm to develop the relationships and, concomitantly, an understanding of the account that larger, more established firms have had for years. It is this aspect of the life of an institutional salesman that makes greatness difficult. Women are in a tough spot in this regard when it comes to sales and, based on my experience, it's tough for women to compete on a truly fair playing field. This isn't due to any inherent lack of drive or interest in the subject matter; it is simply a function of the fact that it's difficult for men and women to be good friends without men misinterpreting friendship as a green light for romantic advances. Like it or not, about 90 percent of a woman's male clients would like to sleep with her, about 50 percent are probably under the delusion that such desires are likely to be reciprocated, and a small but meaningful number will put these two parts of the equation together and try to complete the forward pass. The fact that all women know this and are often less able to determine just which category each one of their male clients might fall into puts the hardworking institutional saleswoman with a conscience at a distinct disadvantage vis-à-vis her male counterparts. This is not unique to Wall Street. This is human nature and millions of years of human evolution at work.

No doubt there are also women who use their beauty and charms as a method of garnering greater and greater commission dollars. This won't work at every account, but it will work at enough of them to tempt the morally agnostic firm to give it a try. One of the most high profile examples of this phenomenon was Danielle Chiesi of Galleon scandal fame, when she used her beauty and her romantic dalliances with corporate executives to obtain inside information. I never met her, but friends who did tell me that she made little secret of the fact that she had seduced clients and would-be tippers of inside information. The fact that she spent fifteen months in a West Virginia correctional facility is a good reason to avoid hiring a woman who would purposefully use her looks as a ploy to deepen her relationships with clients.* When you run a sales organization in a hypercompetitive business, there is periodically the suggestion that you hire the best-looking women you can find that might actually have an interest in our research and in the industry. Being intimately familiar with the mind of the average male, I know there is little doubt that this strategy could be effective—for a while. That is until it results in some sort of scandal whose costs far outweigh the experiment's benefits. More than one Wall Street sales manager has been on the receiving end of phone calls from angry wives of clients who believed things were getting a little too chummy. As long as human beings feel the need to keep up with the Joneses, the customer man's two-front war is likely to continue. But perhaps the financial crisis has reminded both husbands and wives alike that the solutions to life's real problems have no price tag at all.

---

* Every saint has a past, every sinner a future. I wish her well.

7

9/11–THE DAY
EVERYTHING CHANGED

Everyone who had reached the age of reason by September 11, 2001, knows exactly where they were when life in America changed so dramatically. In some ways it was a final, tragic denouement to a twenty-year period of rising affluence and, at times, excess. It was the kind of glorious day one really only gets in Manhattan in September, warm but dry, the azure sky almost divine in its perfection. I was still at ISI and was set to travel with two sales colleagues, Steve and Stephanie, to visit our clients in Boston. As was our custom at the time, we left the office for our nine o'clock shuttle flight after our morning meeting, arriving at the airport at 8:51 a.m. In those days of sleepy security and lax boarding rules we always cut it close and almost never missed a flight. It still amazes me that Steve and I were able to board the plane that day given our tardiness. As the last two guys on the aircraft, we were the kind recipients of the barely concealed hostility of the stewardess in charge.

"You're late," she scolded.

"We know," Steve said apologetically.

"Take your seats now," she said professionally.

In another move reminiscent of the era, my first act upon sitting down was to fire up my cell phone and call the office.

"Hi Rach, it's Jase. What's up?" I asked the firm's reliable sales assistant Rachel.

"Um . . . Something bad just happened at the World Trade Center," she said, sounding somewhat scared. Now with Rachel, "something bad" could have been anything from her breaking a nail to having to break out the paddles to resuscitate one of our colleagues from a heart attack.

"What do you mean 'something bad'?"

"It looks like a plane hit one of the buildings. Oh my God, another one just hit the other tower."

I asked her to put me through to Frank, one of the senior salesmen on our desk.

"Frank, what's up?"

"I don't know what to tell you, Jase. This looks really bad. You might not want to get on that plane. I gotta go." At which point he hung up.

Already having failed to endear myself to the stewardess and over the objections of my far more charming colleague, Steve, I immediately rang the flight attendant button above my seat.

"What?" she asked, now impatient with me.

"Ma'am, it sounds like there's a real problem involving two planes at the World Trade Center. I think you should let the captain know."

She looked at me blankly for a second and then, seeing that I was serious, moved quickly up the aisle. The plane, which was then slowly pulling back from the gate, stopped a minute later. Overhearing my explanation to Steve, others around us started using their cell phones to ascertain the gravity of the situation. Five minutes later, the captain's Southern accent came over the PA system and told us, clinically, that there was a serious airplane accident in downtown Manhattan and that the airline was forced to cancel the flight. While such an announcement would normally be greeted with groans and complaints, nearly everyone on that flight seemed to know by this point that this was the real thing. Five minutes later we arrived back at the gate and were on our own.

Our other colleague on the flight, Stephanie—always a step ahead—had immediately realized that getting a cab from LaGuardia would be impossible and called a car service to bring us back into the city. Nervously, we climbed into the black Lincoln and asked our driver to take us back to our offices on Fifty-fourth and Madison. Sitting in the front seat, I turned on the radio to one of the all-news stations. Within twenty minutes, it seemed, the country had taken on the character of a nation at war. The dispatches from the station's various reporters were alternately reporting accounts of a similar plane attack on the Pentagon and a bomb explosion at the State Department. It was clear that the world had, in some profound way, changed.

Unable to cross the Triborough Bridge, our driver started driving through the excited streets of Queens. Eventually, exasperated by the traffic and having learned that all the bridges and tunnels into Manhattan had been closed, he dejectedly dropped us off at the Queensborough, which enters Manhattan on the East Side at Sixtieth Street, to walk across the span ourselves. On the other side of the bridge, leaving Manhattan, the scene was reminiscent of refugees fleeing the war-torn regions many of us had only witnessed on the six o'clock news. People were using any means necessary to flee the city. There were passenger cars filled with as many as eight, and in one particularly frightening image I really became anxious when I saw what looked like fifty people using a beverage truck with bay doors as a makeshift unarmored personnel carrier. The bridge provided an eerily perfect view of the smoke billowing out of the Towers on the clear, clear late summer day. Having our homes and loved ones in Manhattan, none of us considered staying in Queens. And so we started our trek across the bridge.

Reaching the other side without any ability to use our cellular phones, we told each other to stay safe and went our separate ways. Unable to get in touch with my wife but knowing she worked only a few blocks away from our office in Midtown, I walked across town back to 535 Madison where everyone was glued to the television sets on the trading floor or was looking south down Madison to the Towers. At this point, what had gone on was scary and serious but the Towers were still standing. People were keeping it together. But when one fell and then the second came down at 10:28 a.m., all hell broke loose. Some men and women started to cry while others immediately left the office to start the search for friends and loved ones they knew worked at the World Trade Center, combing area hospitals in the vain hope that anyone caught in the Towers could have survived. After reaching my wife and my parents by e-mail to check on everyone and to assure them that I was safe, I went back to my desk and tried to reach a Georgetown buddy named Tommy Galvin, without success.

Thomas E. Galvin was a senior vice-president as a corporate bond broker at Cantor Fitzgerald and worked on the 104th floor of the North Tower. He was the youngest of four children. He grew up in Greenwich and went on to become the captain of Georgetown's golf team. When he died, Tommy was thirty-two, had a girlfriend, sported a 1.2 handicap, was a member at Winged Foot, and had a great sense of humor and compassion for others. It's hard to believe such a good guy could wake up at six in the morning and be murdered coldly by 10:30 a.m. Knowing it was likely pointless, our group of friends all tried to call his cell phone from our landlines and to e-mail him in the hope that he was still alive. But he was gone. To this day, we all think about him often and always fondly.

The Exchange would remain closed the next day, but given the culture and professionalism of our firm there was little question that we still needed to come to work if at all possible. While we couldn't execute any trades, we, like all of our competitors, had to help our clients make sense of this tragedy and offer some insight into how things might move forward.

I started to write a report for our clients to be published the following day, Thursday, the thirteenth of September. "There is obviously no true historical precedent for Tuesday's horrific tragedy," I wrote. "But the market's performance after the following events may provide some perspective for investors." After that I—somewhat coldly now that I think about it—highlighted the market's reaction after Pearl Harbor, the Cuban Missile Crisis, the assassination of President Kennedy, and Iraq's invasion of Kuwait.

Ed offered whatever extra space we had to our clients that were displaced by the war zone that had become the financial district and a number of our colleagues wound up rooming with friends who lived uptown.

Mercifully, this was the only time in my life when I experienced the collective grief of a metropolitan area with twelve million people. All Americans mourned of course, but it was personal if you lived in New York, had family and friends who were cops or firemen, or worked on Wall Street. The tentacles of the tragedy extended far and wide and I daresay that I didn't know anyone who hadn't lost someone on 9/11. The sadness was everywhere for months upon months and it wasn't unusual for some of the living to have to attend dozens of memorial services for fallen friends and family. Memorials to those who perished can be found everywhere in Manhattan and its environs. Everyone's perspective changed that day, most especially those of us on Wall Street. September 11 was a tragic bookend to an era in which the delusion of mass happiness, so present in America in the 1990s, was thought to be endlessly sustainable. It wasn't.

8

PUNDIT, POET, DRINKER, DINER

It was 6:00 a.m. on a snowy February morning in 2010. Two Wall Street professionals, of whom I was one, sat in a rented Ford Flex outside the Hilton in Fort Wayne, Indiana.

"So what's the story, Todd?"

"We have a meeting with the bank's clients in Warsaw."

"Indiana or Poland?"

"It's about an hour away off the highway at a place called Noa Noa—a steak house. Caribbean, I think. About fifty people will be there."

"So let me get this straight. In an hour, I'm going to give a speech to fifty people at a Caribbean steakhouse in Warsaw, Indiana."

"Yep."

"Given the venue, does the fact that it's six in the fuckin' morning and it's nine degrees strike you as the least bit strange?"

"Don't forget to wear your seat belt," he said, ignoring my mini tantrum. We were off.

Near-constant travel has led me to try to find the blessings inherent in what could easily be viewed as a curse. One of the things I've learned in my career is that it's hard to be a true contrarian when one lives and works in Manhattan. Despite its pretension of cosmopolitanism and open-mindedness, this island can lead even the most seasoned pro into one of the easiest, and yet perhaps most dangerous, traps in the investment business—the confidence that one is contrarian when one is solidly in the consensus. As Mark Twain once said, "It ain't what you don't know that gets you into trouble; it's what you know for sure that just ain't so." As I've discussed, it is often the nonconsensus ideas—those seen almost heretical—that yield the greatest returns. Almost by definition, the trades you are more convinced are correct cause the greatest losses. As we whizzed past Waffle Houses and car dealers and mobile home communities on our straight-as-an-arrow drive on US 30 that February morning, I started to think about what an incredible country America is. The idea that fifty people would get up before the sun rose, braving snow and ice and single-digit temperatures to listen to another "expert" from New York is still mystifying and humbling to me. As is always the case when I'm asked to speak to clients of the local bank's trust department, I still marvel at the businesses and the wealth these people without pretense have built despite what other experts on the coasts have done to them. The opportunity to meet people in all parts of this great country is both a personal privilege and a professional advantage for the serious student of economics and the financial markets. It is all the more important and necessary if one lives on the Fantasy Island we call Manhattan.

I live in a town where a lot of people think, still, that they are masters of the universe and that the rest of us are merely satellites who revolve around them. When you visit the heartland, it's hard not to be reminded of Warren Buffett's famous quip that Wall Street is the only place where a man who takes the subway might dispense advice to a man who rides around in a Rolls-Royce. This was obvious the instant we started chatting up the crowd at Noa Noa in Warsaw, Indiana.

On the way out, my hosts let me in on who I was actually talking to—that the man in the Christmas sweater and the duck boots built a great fortune in the corrugated box business or that the kind old lady eating her scrambled eggs in the front row owns one of the largest independent trucking companies in the Midwest. The guy in the flannel shirt is an eye surgeon and has built his wealth through the slow, steady, and prudent application of his expertise. These people aren't quick-buck artists and yet they could buy and sell the vast majority of Wall Street hotshots who might compete with one another on the price they paid for their watch.

After five years running ISI's company surveys business Monday through Friday and moonlighting, largely without permission, as the firm's strategist once a month for a few years, I had begun to lobby Ed for more responsibility. I wanted to assume the sell-side title of chief investment strategist—an important, or at least prestigious, role in any research firm. My opinions about the markets would be given more weight and I would work more closely with Ed to set the overall research forecast for the firm. I was a little young for the job at such a good firm but the success of the company survey effort and my pestering led Ed eventually to give in. This was my chance at the "show." It was an incredible chance at Wall Street "stardom" such as it was defined and, like many good things in my life, it was made possible by men under no obligation to help me. Ed Hyman probably couldn't take my constant entreaties for him to give me the job any longer. And two other men, Jim Moltz, whom I'll talk about later, and the legendary strategist Byron Wien, gave me one of the greatest gifts of all—encouragement.

Byron, the éminence grise of the investment strategy community and perhaps the most celebrated writer in Wall Street history, had a big influence on my career. He had been a legendary strategist at Morgan Stanley for two decades when I first met him in person at a Georgetown alumni event in the late 1990s to discuss his famed "Ten Investment Surprises." Although his regular musings on the global economy, on the financial markets, and on geopolitics are among the most widely followed investment research pieces in the world, he became famous for an elegant investment piece based on the insight that most great investments are the result of a variant perception from what the consensus believes. The device was an immediate marketing hit and ultimately the basis for our friendship. In his speech, I found him to be erudite, candid, and kind. I wrote him a note asking humbly what he thought about ten investment surprises I had developed on my own, imitation being the sincerest form of flattery. To my amazement, he not only wrote back words of encouragement but he also invited me to lunch. He was a superstar, I a lowly upstart, but he urged me to pursue my desire to become a strategist in my own right and we've remained friends ever since. Perhaps I was wrong. Maybe it was just before you had actually achieved something that no one on Wall Street would help you out. After a decade in the trenches some of the professionals that had seemed so flinty to you in the past now seemed to soften.

My respect for the man only grew when I learned that he wasn't born the fully formed Wall Street hero I first met at the height of the nineties bull market. A native of Chicago, he had struggled far more than I have had to, and his story is truly inspiring. After being orphaned at the age of fourteen (his father died when he was nine, his mother five years later) his academic record earned him a place reserved for public school students at Harvard, where he wrote for the *Crimson*. After receiving his MBA, also in

Cambridge, he spent some time in advertising, in the army, and in management consulting. The investment world was blessed when a classmate of his asked him to join Weiss, Peck, and Greer, a small but successful investment management firm, as a security analyst. After what he describes as a fitful start, he developed into a star portfolio manager at the firm and, after twenty-one years, was tapped by Barton Biggs, then Morgan Stanley chief investment officer, to head the investment strategy team at Morgan Stanley in 1984. There has been only one major career, market, or business decision I have made in the past twenty years without consulting Byron—and that was to start my own firm. He only once asked me why I never asked him about it and I told him frankly that I feared that he, being an exceptionally intelligent and rational human being, would have tried to talk me out of it. He didn't disagree.

Byron was a very important inspiration to me as a strategist in another way. He demonstrated regularly and to the great benefit of his clients that a love of letters could be a great asset as a strategist. Drawing widely on every part of his education, Byron writes about the markets with a humanity that attracts the interests and attentions of the professional who arguably has more to read than any other—the institutional investor. I was blessed to have grown up in a book-filled household in which the great writers were revered and regularly discussed. Having just turned eighty, he vowed never to retire, much to the benefit of Blackstone's institutional investment clients and his many friends throughout the world.

I patterned my own professional writing after Byron's, and as I started to do some public punditry in the late 1990s, I began to read widely and voraciously a range of great writers, especially the ones who wrote about other activities that might break your heart—sports and war—with the hope of turning what could be dry reports into something other people might actually want to read. H. L. Mencken, A. J. Liebling, Grantland Rice, Ernie Pyle, Oriana Fallaci, Damon Runyon, and Hunter S. Thompson all served as models in those years. In the process I learned the importance of telling stories: while the tape may be boring at times, the characters of this business never are.

In any event, those first few years on the road as an analyst were great ones, mainly because my entire preoccupation became my occupation. Although I had an assistant, conducting the company surveys while at the same time reading and writing research and visiting clients was challenging. As a strategist, I could focus more on reading the work of others and had more time to think when I wasn't in front of clients. The travel became a considerably more inconvenient and at times frightening experience in the aftermath of 9/11, but I was making a name for myself, hungrily reading everything I could about the markets, and constantly learning from the questions asked by my institutional clients on the road. It was in those days that I realized how important the travel was to my actual research. On every trip a question would be asked that required further study and thought. My findings back at the home office with my trusted lieutenant, Nick Bohnsack, and under the tutelage and guidance of Jim Moltz, then provided the raw materials for our next report, the key question asked on the road invariably one that other clients had as well.

But the life of a sell sider can be physically brutal. It isn't uncommon on these trips to be perpetually exhausted, and it doesn't get any easier as you get older. A trip to Dallas and Houston, for example, generally entails no less than ten one-on-one meetings in addition to a group luncheon, dinner, or breakfast. After traveling for a while you have no desire to spend more time away from home than you have to, and even if you wanted to, your wife and your boss wouldn't let you. The focus then is in being as efficient with your travel time as possible. This generally means that you're on the first flight out in the morning. Up at 4:00 a.m. to make a 6:00 a.m. flight, what little sleep you get on the plane involves physical contortions that render it useless. Once you land, your day starts with a series of meetings wherein you more or less give the same stump speech so often you could do it without thinking. Your paying clients deserve and require you to be on, to be thoughtful and entertaining, and to do your best to answer questions for which there are sometimes no good answers.

This isn't to say there weren't times when I enjoyed the travel and the opportunities to entertain, especially when I later became an analyst. It wasn't uncommon to visit Paris, Zurich, Milan, and Tokyo every year. But the truth of the matter was that you were just as likely to have to visit Jackson, Mississippi, in August and Anchorage in February if you weren't a partner. After the first three years, the glamour wore off and the only thing that made a real difference was the competence and sense of humor of the salesman with whom you were traveling. Strategists and economists are a somewhat different breed of sell-side analyst. Perhaps because their work is sometimes felt to be more in the realm of entertainment than serious research, we often see institutional salesmen, correctly, as our greatest allies in the circuit of capturing the mindshare of portfolio managers and analysts. Consequently, it is not uncommon for the young strategist or technician to be used as a legitimate front for what are often boondoggles and other wasteful forms of travel and entertainment.*

On one trip with Jack, a straight-out-of-Central-Casting institutional salesman, we somehow managed to find three custom-

---

* In one famous incident Bear Stearns had been sued for a wayward forecast on bonds by its chief economist. The firm's defense was, laughably, that no experienced investor would ever rely on the predictions of a Wall Street economist.

ers in New Orleans who were willing to trade with us. The irony of course is that the amount of money used to entertain these guys in any given year probably exceeded any revenues they might provide. Jack didn't care and why should he; he was paid on the top line. Our annual trip there was unjustifiable in almost every way and if it were a television series would have been titled *Businessmen Gone Wild*. Our clients knew where to find the best bands and where the bars would tend to our needs with alacrity. New Orleans remains one of the few places on the planet where you can really lose track of time and where grown men and women with families routinely stay out all night. Being a little bit older, at thirty-two, more senior in the organization, and married, I found myself in the position of being "mature" when I decided to retire at 3:00 a.m. during one such trip. Our hosts were native New Orleanians with French surnames, charming Southern accents, and some of the greatest Mardi Gras stories ever told.

"Jack," I said. "I'll see you tomorrow morning. I've gotta get out of here if I have any chance of making any sense at our meetings. You going to be OK?"

Jack laughed and said, "See you tomorrow in the lobby at eight thirty a.m., sport. We'll be fine."

Somewhat self-satisfied that I was acting responsibly, I got four hours of sleep and showed up at the appointed hour and place to drive to our first meeting, about an hour's drive away. I didn't become anxious about making our 10:00 a.m. meeting until about 8:45—still no Jack. My head pounding, and beads of sweat rolling off my forehead, I really started to worry about ten minutes later. I was in a full state of panic at 9:05 a.m. when Jack rolled up in a taxi with "Montana," one of the previous night's "performance artists." He walked into the hotel, saw me, clearly agitated, and said, chuckling, "Don't worry, sport. I'll be down in a few minutes."

Left there to stew, I realized it was my own fault for being talked into this trip in the first place. Forty minutes later, Jack walked downstairs, retrieved our rental car, and we were off to a meeting for which we would be at least forty-five minutes late.

"Don't worry," he said, taking the wheel and clearly sensing my anger. "These guys are used to it. I already called ahead."

After about a quarter of a mile, Jack pulled off to the side of the road and stopped.

"Whatsa matter, Jack?" I asked excitedly.

"Jase?" he said, sheepishly.

"Yeah."

"I'm really in no condition to drive."

A nervous silence descended over the car. I wasn't Jack's boss but I had a fancy title and there was little doubt that I was supposed to be the more responsible one of the two.

"Jack, are you kiddin' me? We're already going to be late and I'm not exactly a hundred percent myself. If we get pulled over, I'll be the one in trouble."

"Well," he said, "I don't know what to tell you. If we don't make these meetings, then this whole trip would have really been a waste of time," somehow parrying the collective responsibility to our clients solely on my shoulders. This was a little rich coming from a guy who still had last night's glitter on his face and smelled like jasmine.

"OK," I said, sighing, getting out of the car, and taking the wheel.

We arrived about an hour late and our portfolio manager host was unnecessarily gracious.

"Sorry we're late," Jack said, bounding into the reception area of the office. "You know the traffic, it was a mess."

But what the portfolio manager would be too kind to point out, the trading desk at the account would not. As we stopped by to see the traders on our way out, they knew, intuitively, why we weren't on time.

"Look at these guys!" one of the traders said. "They spent a little too much time in the Quarter last night!"

"Yeah, these guys can't control themselves down here," said another. "The only thing this guy's missin'," he said, pointing to me, the suntanned guy in the pinstriped suit, "is a violin case."

It served us right. We violated one of the cardinal rules of the sales and trading game. Players play hurt. No tears. Whatever trouble you found yourself the night before, you're expected to show up and bring your clients the investment research insights and forecasts for which you were paid. This was true no matter what part of the business you happened to be in. When I was on the FX desk at Merrill, this sometimes meant leaving the Ear Inn only to go home, take a shower, shave, and return immediately to work.

It was also in those years that I started to enjoy another part of the life of the modern Wall Street sell-side analyst—the ability to satisfy one's need for fifteen minutes of fame by being on television. While I can't say that Ed was ever that enthusiastic about my frequent television appearances, I can say that he never tried to stop me. Ed was from an era in which, apart from Lou Rukeyser's *Wall Street Week* on Friday nights, regularly appearing on financial television was antithetical to running a for-profit research effort. And how did you decide what you could talk about and what was proprietary to your business? But the times were changing and by the mid-1990s CNBC had made more than a few Wall Street analysts stars. How much impact these shows had on our business is still hard to gauge, but as a strategist just starting out, I have little doubt that it was helpful to my career when I first started appearing regularly in 1998 in the midst of one of the most fantastic bull markets in history.

My first appearance came on the now defunct CNNfn, then the only real competitor to CNBC. I was almost as nervous as my father who, my mom later told me, couldn't bear to watch the potential meltdown of his only son. In my first lesson in the superficiality of the medium, I tried, a little like Nixon in the first televised presidential debate, to eschew makeup. I'm no Mel Gibson—I'm not even Charlie Gibson—and avoiding makeup led me to the same fate Tricky Dick suffered in 1960. I looked pale and sickly, no small task for someone who gets tanned from fluorescent lighting. I gave in almost immediately after watching the videotapes of my first few appearances and found that, just like everyone else, I was primarily concerned with the permanent tea bags under my eyes and the mole on the left side of my nose rather than the cogency of any argument I happened to be making. High-definition television has made the situation all the worse in recent years; small flaws can make a grotesque caricature of anyone.

Like everyone else who's willing to risk humiliation, I got the hang of it over time and in the ensuing years wound up appearing on everything from CNBC, Fox Business, Bloomberg, Yahoo TV, to even CNBC Italia. Part of what allowed me to face my fear of failure was the joint realization that few of my clients were actually listening to what I had to say (unless it's a national emergency, the sound in trading rooms is almost always turned off) and that a typical twenty-four-hour news network might host 150 guests on any given day. Television appearances, truth be told, are important for building a firm's brand, especially with individual investors. It raised my profile, which many of our salesmen liked. I've averaged about forty television appearances every year since then and at least half the comments from friends, family, and clients have more to do with how I look (almost always tired) than what I have to say.

After a while I was asked to start guest hosting shows for

CNBC, Bloomberg, and Fox. This opportunity gives you considerably more time to comment on economic and market trends that are often pointless to try to discuss in sound bites.

About the time I was initiated into the world of television, my career advanced to the point where I underwent another flattering experience, but one with a sand trap I didn't avoid. A rite of passage for any sell-side analyst is the effort and indignity associated with the yearly rankings conducted by *Institutional Investor* magazine. The publication routinely surveys Wall Street's largest institutional investors to determine its rankings of analysts in over fifty industries worldwide. It may not sound like a big deal to be ranked as the number one Wall Street analyst covering, for example, nonferrous metals, but at many large brokerage houses high rankings are tied to compensation, especially if the sector happens to be important to the investment banking division's ability to underwrite initial public offerings and secondaries of securities. The conflicts of interest become obvious to anyone who's ever worked in a brokerage firm for more than five minutes. Can an analyst really be expected to give his or her honest opinion about a company that has contracted their firm to sell the company's securities or for which it hopes to do so sometime in the future? The crisis point for this unholy alliance took place in the late 1990s, when Wall Street firms were competing with such enthusiasm for new IPO business during the Internet boom that it was typical for highly ranked analysts to receive offers from competing firms well into seven figures.

The irony in all of this was that many of the companies in the hot Internet sector were impossible to value by any traditional method of securities analysis that relied on such standard pedestrian metrics as sales, profits, profit margins, or, can you imagine, dividends. In perhaps one of the most embarrassing episodes for

an industry that is no stranger to them, investigators and regulators found e-mails and other damning evidence of analysts' bla-
tant disregard for the truth about the companies they were covering
in order to curry favor with other companies they wanted to do
investment banking with. More than one analyst privately described a company as a POS (piece of shit) in an e-mail while
publicly extolling the company's virtues and rating its stock a
"buy." Some analysts did it for the money, others to be considered
team players, and, in the most notorious instance, an unscrupu-
lous analyst did it to get his kids into an exclusive Manhattan pre-
school. The revelations led to an avalanche of new regulations
and, for some high-profile analysts, lifetime bans from the securities industry.

Unsurprisingly, fewer than 1 percent of sell-side analyst rec-
ommendations on stocks are actually rated a "sell." And so, the
annual *Institutional Investor* (or *II*) rankings remain an extremely
subjective way of determining just who the best analysts on Wall
Street really are. The lengths to which analysts will go to get recognized range from countless phone calls and travel during "voting season" in the spring to other unnuanced methods of garnering
attention just shy of skywriting extravaganzas. This desperation
would be humorous if the stakes weren't so high—especially when
you're a young analyst trying to make sure your bosses won't replace you with a more highly ranked competitor. As the owner of
my own brokerage firm today, I have the luxury of ignoring the
rankings, choosing instead to focus on growing our business with
a far more objective measure of success—money.

But then—in my early thirties, when I was still trying to establish my bona fides as a chief investment strategist for an important firm like ISI—I was just as shameless as everyone else. My
telephone seemed to be an outgrowth of my Lilliputian ears and
I racked up tens of thousands of frequent-flier miles. It took me

three years to break into the top echelon of Wall Street strategists according to *Institutional Investor*'s poll, but when the rankings came out in October 2003, there I was, listed in the top six on a list of something approaching a hundred sell-side strategists. Ed Hyman knew how important this milestone was for me and in a characteristically generous gesture bought the other ranked analysts at the firm and me silver Rolexes with *II 2003* inscribed on the back. It was a good day—a symbol of vindication for a lot of hard work, late nights, missed connections, and five-hour flights spent in middle, economy-class seats. In the cab on the way to my apartment that October evening, I called home to share the good news with my mom and dad.

"Ma, you know that industry poll I told you about? Well, I got ranked and the company bought me a Rolex in recognition."

"Really," my mother said excitedly. "That's great. Now you can organize all your contacts and those business cards in one place. That's terrific."

It took me a second but I remembered that my parents were from a different era.

"No, Ma, not a Rolodex—a *Rolex*, you know, the watch."

"Oh," she said, somewhat deflated. "Well, that's nice too. But don't you already have a watch?"

For Depression-era babies, a Rolodex would forever be a far more practical gift than a fancy Swiss timepiece. Still, it represented a lot of what I had been striving for all those years. After time in the back office, being a rookie salesman, starting all over again in business school, and realizing that I was never going to be a great trader, my ability to meet famed Wall Street stars, to travel, and to garner some recognition for my efforts publicly and privately was some validation of my hard work.

* * *

After a few years of being "out there," traveling extensively and doing the financial television circuit, I started to attract the attention of other Wall Street firms, most notably Bear Stearns. While I was happy in my ISI position at the time, the extensive travel and the stress of working at a small firm had started to grate. The possibility of being named the chief investment strategist at a large firm also, I must admit, appealed to my vanity. At the time, Bear Stearns—more than any other Wall Street firm—knew how to game the *Institutional Investor* ranking process and claimed with some justification that it could make any good analyst number one in his or her industry. A fellow Georgetown alumnus, Tom Bianco, reached out to me and, after a series of interviews with the associate director of research, Barbara Reguero, with the director of research, Kay Booth, and with a number of the firm's other economists and strategists, I was offered the big job at a salary 50 percent higher than what I was earning at ISI. A slight catch was that 25 to 35 percent of my earnings were to be paid in restricted stock at the firm's discretion. In other words, what on paper looked like a big payout was largely in control of the firm for three years. I was flattered, but I now faced a dilemma: stay with a small company that gave me a chance, where I knew just about everything and everybody, or leap into the great unknown of a large and publicly traded brokerage firm with vast global resources. The Bear job would be far more high profile but it would also carry far more risk: both my successes and my failures would be magnified at a firm that had a reputation for sharp elbows. Restricted stock grants also made the raise in pay somewhat more of an abstraction, especially since it was well known that the firm discouraged its employees from ever selling the stock, once vested.

I talked to Ed about the offer and gave him my reasons for considering the move. What happened next still surprises me. Ed offered to double my salary and fly first-class when needed. Ultimately, it wasn't that difficult a decision. I liked the job and I wanted to finish what I started with people I knew and liked rather than take a chance at a large shop where office politics would in no small measure determine my fate.

Now I had to tell Bear Stearns about my decision. Unfortunately, this wasn't my greatest moment. The manner in which I declined Bear's offer—via e-mail—left much to be desired with regard to corporate etiquette and class. It was the coward's way of avoiding a difficult conversation. Tom Bianco, Barbara Reguero, and Kay Booth were all understandably angry. After an hour-long harangue from Tom about the classlessness of my behavior, Bear's head of equities, Bruce Lisman, called me at home to express his own disappointment. Ultimately he said, "Jason, if you ask me, this whole episode and the way you've handled it is just wacko."

He was right. But it was more than just wacko; it was wrong. The whole affair was yet another example, as St. Teresa of Avila pointed out, that often more tears are shed over answered prayers than unanswered ones. Bear's ultimate demise as an independent firm in March 2008 destroyed tens of millions of dollars of wealth for many employees who had devoted their lives to the company. Once again, I got lucky.

Those years as an ISI strategist were often extraordinarily fun, but eventually they started to come with a heavy cost—too much distance from a young family, and a physical and mental exhaustion that had my friends and family worried about my health. By early 2006, I was ready for a change.

9

MY OWN SHOP

I remember the instant I decided to start my own firm. It was in 2005, during another marathon trip that included stops in Seattle, Portland, Vancouver, and Alaska—a Bataan Death March with snow. My epiphany arrived on a particularly bad night at the Hotel Alaskan in Anchorage. It was February and freezing and as luck would have it, some jackass had set off a fire drill in the middle of the night. At three in the morning, I awoke to find that there was also no electricity. Stumbling around a room in the kind of total darkness that can only be found in the wilderness, I somehow found a camper's lamp whose light enabled me to get dressed and find my way to the parking lot to await a sign that things were safe. At a certain point I heard a familiar voice among the shadows. "Jase, is that you?" I raised the lamp to the stranger's face in medieval fashion. It was Hank, the salesman with whom I was traveling. The absurdity of our predicament and my use of the lamp made us laugh the way you do only in times of fateful misery. A few hours later, I walked across the tarmac under the umbrella of a dark and frigid Alaskan morning and dutifully took my seat for the flight to Vancouver. The boarding not yet complete and the door of the plane open, I was wedged into seat 3A of a prop plane, cold, miserable, compressing stool at two hundred pounds per square inch. I couldn't help but wonder aloud, "Why?" What's the point? My dad had passed away eight months before, I was drinking too much, and I felt as if I had no control over my own schedule. I was fighting a two-front war and hopelessly trapped between the needs of a hungry sales force and the emotional needs of my young family. Jerry Maguire–like, I felt there had to be a better way—fewer clients, more research, less travel, more thought, and more control.

There were many compensations of course: the train trip in the snow from Zurich to Zug to visit Marc Rich's firm; the speech in Rome, in Italian, just before Christmas and the four days with my wife that followed; the meetings with some of the world's great investment minds—George Soros, Julian Robertson, Barton Biggs, Bill Gross, Byron Wien, Lee Cooperman, and scores of other famous and purposefully anonymous investors. These perks along with the money kept you going. The problem about life on the sell side, however, was that the positive impact on your psyche of these experiences tended to diminish over time. You needed more and more money and approbation to outweigh what always remained—the physical exhaustion, the stress, the time away from your family, and a complete lack of control over your own life.

By any standard, I was well paid for my work and, for the most part, well treated by the firm's partners. But still, I couldn't help feeling a vulnerability about my career that seemed greatly inconsistent with what I believed to be my contributions to the firm. Although it can be argued that it was of limited commercial value, I was largely the face of ISI in the media. I had also built two important research products for the company. And after fifteen years, I didn't think it made sense that I had no equity in the firm or even, for that matter, a contract. I was an at-will employee just like everyone else. My experiences with people at Morgan Stanley and Merrill led me to believe that there would be no loyalty to me if I happened to have a bad run. These are the things that run through your brain when you're freezing your ass off in a prop plane in Alaska helping build another man's business. "You can't eat the orange and throw the peel away—a man is not a piece of fruit."*

Turgenev once famously commented that a boy doesn't become a man until he loses a father. My decision to venture out on my own was also heightened by the loss of my dad, a man who suppressed all of his personal ambitions for my development. He passed away in July 2005 of prostate cancer.

After a two-year stint in the army during which, according to his account, his main preoccupation was "chasing broads in Stuttgart," he taught English and poetry for thirty-four years at my alma mater, Hauppauge High School on Long Island. My father was one of those rare types who could speak with equal ease and passion to the guy on his right about Faulkner or Milton and to the guy on his left about Conn or Furillo. We all create our own realities in a sense and the world my dad inhabited led him to live by his unique code wherein pride mattered more than money and the popular media didn't cheapen real tragedies or give people virtually limitless "second acts." My father accepted other people's faults and imperfections, and he abhorred phonies of any type. He loved baseball, boxing, and horseracing, and he adored dogs. These may seem strange interests for a poet, but I believe that for him there was a certain honesty in sport—a score or a time—and an innocence in animals that provided him a welcome refuge from man's petulance and venality.

My dad did very little lecturing to me as I was growing up. But there was one time, during a rare but almost clichéd high

---

* Arthur Miller, *Death of a Salesman*, Act 2.

school indiscretion when we sat across from each other at the kitchen table and he said to me, in a quiet rage, "We're not like the other people. We don't sail through life. Our mistakes have *consequences*." And it was at once that I saw, even at that age, that this was a man of a different generation who had, despite his advanced education (or was it because of it?), a deep respect for the Fates. The defining moment in my dad's life was the sudden and tragic loss of his own father when he was only sixteen. His poetry talked about that and the other vicissitudes of luck that could derail the plans of the common man. I have no idea whether my father's poems were any good, but to me they are exceptional.

My dad and I were very close and talked about just about everything, except, until it was probably too late, the seriousness of his illness. We cared about each other too much to dwell on that and our rare silences probably said all that needed to be said about such morbidities.

Even confronted with his own mortality, he found great solace in poetry. In those final weeks he rediscovered Francis Thompson's searingly beautiful "The Hound of Heaven," with Sister Joyce.

As strange as it may sound, some good was derived from my father's passing. In a weird way I found it liberating, because his death was sufficiently sad for me to feel I had the right for the first time since I was married to be selfish. I had an overwhelming desire to spend more time doing things I liked with people I respected and less time doing frivolous things with inconsequential people I didn't like (debating things like whether we should bring chocolate pretzels rather than fruit to off-site meetings with clients, for example).

My father's death also brought home how impersonal my business can be. I was struck by the complete indifference and insensitivity some of the people in my firm displayed after my dad died. Death is a part of life, and business is business. I knew that but it

hurt and I found myself angry. I thought about the weeks of my
life spent with our self-important salesman covering Europe, the
interminable conversations I had with middle management about
their athletic and romantic exploits in college, and all the 6:00 a.m.
flights to places far and wide. But virtually nobody except Jim
Moltz said a word to me about my father. Obviously, my old man's
death was unremarkable, a simple yet sad rite of passage for all of
us. He didn't need to be idolized in death but still I thought that
"attention must finally be paid to such a person."*

A great friend from high school put it this way when his
mother passed away: "Your life just stops but everyone else's just
moves on." I wanted to believe that people I worked with cared a
little bit more for me and not just what I could do for them. I was
no great character, no saint, but I tried. I went to church, did my
best for my firm and my family, and made a concerted effort not
to hurt anyone.

But I saw myself getting old in my late thirties, feeling more
and more like one of those burnt-out cops in the movies who just
has to turn in his shield. And whatever ability I had to offer insights on the movements of the financial markets was slowly being eaten away by a hungry sales force, staff meetings, and the
red-eye to Frankfurt. After twelve years on the road and a fair
amount of success, money, and media exposure, I was worn out
and knew I needed a change. I knew too that the two-front war I
complained about wasn't helped by my penchant for getting ham-
mered with the sales guys or going to strip clubs or spending
$3,000 for a suit from Naples or eating steak three times a week.
For more than two decades, I willingly participated in and enjoyed
the trappings of an adolescent's view of what life on Wall Street
was supposed to be like. But on vacation I began to find myself

---

* Arthur Miller, *Death of a Salesman*, Act 1.

envious of people with relatively uncomplicated jobs that involved physical labor. At least in such jobs the complaints about my work and my boss might seem valid. And at least then I could dream about the *possibility* of being able to afford all the things I took for granted now. I started to realize for the first time that the greatest pleasures in life lie in their anticipation.

What possesses men and women with good jobs to leave and start new ventures fraught with risk will remain one of the great mysteries of this country. It was somewhat more curious in my case because in many ways I genuinely enjoyed my job, became friends with the vast majority of my co-workers, loved the interactions with our clients, respected my bosses, and was well compensated. But a trip to visit Cincinnati for a CFA dinner led to a chance encounter with a dean of the investment strategy business named Bob and sealed my fate as an aspiring entrepreneur.

"Let me ask you a question," he said. "You ever get sick of the travel, shitty club food like this, and giving the same pitch ten times a day?"

The question shocked me because I thought it was obvious to anyone involved that the answer was an unequivocal yes. But it wasn't rhetorical. Bob had done what I did for a living for the better part of twenty years for a large money-center bank as one of its international economists and I got the sense that he wanted to know whether his feelings about a life on the road were somehow odd. He was smart and friendly and I remember feeling relieved when we were on panels or in the media together.

"I wanted to get out of that racket when I had two boys," he continued. "Then my wife said she wanted a little girl. I resisted, and I still don't know how this happened, but she got pregnant again. The little girl wound up being two twin boys. I was happy of course but any chance of moving out of the fast lane evaporated. I missed some good years trying to catch the five thirty train from Ridgewood and jetting all around the globe," he said, his voice trailing. "But it worked out in the end. We're all buddies now. I'm just happy they're not in this business."

Again no one's going to shed crocodile tears for Bob. He had a great sell-side career and successfully made the transition to chief investment officer of an insurance company. Still, it was a glimpse into my future that was jarring, and somewhat frightening. I was then thirty-eight, had a little money in the bank, and could list as dependents only one wife and one son. It turned out to be something of a fool's paradise but I hoped that starting my own firm would afford me a little less time traveling, a little more time with my family, more time to write and to think, and a lower handicap. I also wondered, in sooth, whether I was slowly becoming a phony. One of the ironies of the sell-side research business is that the more widely your work is followed the less time you have to do research. It seemed almost dishonest to spend countless hours holding forth my views about the economy and criticizing corporate America without ever having to sign the front side of a paycheck myself. I still travel too much for my liking and my handicap is still hopelessly mired at 17.5 but I did get more control over my life and that, combined with my wife's decision to stop working, made an enormous difference at home. The two-front war disappeared. For the most part, I only have to watch my right flank from 7:00 a.m. to 6:00 p.m. Monday through Friday these days.

Having finally made the decision to venture out on my own, I then started to seek out others interested in creating our own firm. Nick Bohnsack, my right-hand man and a talented strategist in his own right, was immediately interested. We shared our plan with Don Rissmiller, a young but extraordinarily gifted economist at our firm, over whiskey and cigars in a surreptitious meeting at Club Macanudo on Sixty-third and Madison. While there was little doubt that we would have been summarily shitcanned and embarrassed if our plans had been discovered, there were precious few cloak-and-dagger maneuvers during the preparations to start our own business. It became almost immediately apparent to me that building a new firm was going to become an infinitely more expensive, yet far more useful form of an MBA. We also learned in short order that the word "expedite" might be the most expensive word in the English language and wondered why children don't have nightmares about lawyers rather than big hairy monsters.

Informing the partners of our firm of our decision to start a new firm in August 2006 was by far the most stressful day of my business career. Having spent the better part of fifteen years at the firm, I knew that whatever modest success I had enjoyed was due in large measure to its misplaced leaps of faith and support of me. I had learned the business of sell-side research from Ed, who knew it better than anyone. His great insight as a Wall Street analyst was the realization that his customers wanted research that distinguished itself by its utility rather than its theoretical scholarship. I'd learned the great importance, and challenge, of making difficult concepts simple. His charts and data would often be accompanied with lines and arrows and exclamations like WOW! and SURPRISING! to underscore his points for people who had too much to read. He did this at a time when Wall Street economists took themselves even more seriously than they do today. I once heard a jealous competitor refer to his work as a "cartoon service for the great ERISA unwashed." Ultimately, I was deathly afraid of having my decision be seen as a betrayal to a man who had given me such great opportunities.

After our morning meeting, I walked to Ed's desk on the edge of the trading floor to tell him the news. Although I had been preparing for this moment for some time I was shaking. Sensing bad news, he looked up and I asked him if we could chat privately. It felt as if the entire firm knew and once we repaired to a conference room, I said as quickly and simply as possible that I thought it was time for me to start my own firm. There was obvious disappointment but no yelling and no drama. He asked for some time to discuss it with senior members of the firm but after some back and forth I convinced him that I wasn't doing this for more money or power or prestige. It was simply time to go.

Ultimately, he asked me why I wanted to leave a firm that had been so good to me. I gave him the most honest answer I could muster.

"Ed, I really just want to be like you. I think it's time I captain my own ship."

While there were undoubtedly a few tense moments in our final two weeks, Ed, a true believer in the wisdom of free markets, appreciated the answer and engineered as graceful and amicable an exit from the firm as could have been expected under the circumstances. In some instances, such departures can be nasty, with harsh words and threats of lawsuits exchanged. I know this is something that would never have happened at any of the other firms I had worked at, and I remain grateful that the transition from employee to small businessman wasn't any more traumatic than it had to be.

On my last day, I was reminded of what I still believe to be one of the great novels of the twentieth century, Lampedusa's *The Leopard,* as singularly beautiful in English as it is in Italian. The novel takes place in Sicily during the Risorgimento and its main protagonist, Don Fabrizio, a Sicilian prince, is forced to confront what will be the inevitable decline of his influence in a unified Italy. His favorite nephew, Tancredi, offers the book's central paradox: "*Se vogliamo che tutto rimanga come e', bisogna che tutto cambi.*" If we wish for everything to stay the same, everything must change.

Predictably, my new partners and my old friends from the firm met at Rothmann's after work to say our good-byes. There were no tears but few laughs. We all knew that our relationships with one another wouldn't be the same for a long time. I was leaving friends I had developed over my entire working career; our venture was hardly a sure thing.

We worked quickly to get our new firm up and running, publishing our first piece less than a month later on September 6, 2006. The capital we had to put up represented a not insignificant portion of our own respective net worth. For 10 percent of our new firm, we received some start-up capital from former Citigroup executives Bobby DiFazio, Bobby Moore, and Bill Heinzerling. Pulse, a small Boston-based brokerage firm with offices in New York, rented us their conference room at a reduced rate to capture our trading flow and, mercy of mercies, we were able to convince Eileen Gallocher and Katarina Lundberg from our old shop to join us as office manager and research director respectively. A week after we gave our two weeks' notice, Nick and I took one of our most important mentors, Jim Moltz, ISI's vice-chairman and former CEO of C. J. Lawrence and board member of the New York Stock Exchange, out for lunch to ask his advice as we were about to get started. I'll talk more about Jim later in the book, but for now, I'll just say that we put as much stock into what he told us as anyone. As we took our seats at the restaurant, we were apologetic about our decision to leave a firm that had been good to us. Through a wry smile he said simply, "It's forever been thus." As far as advice, he provided two simple admonitions that have served us well ever since. "First," he said, "keep your fixed costs as low as possible. When I was running C. J. in the seventies and eighties we would make projections about our revenues every year and every year they were hopelessly off. We learned quickly that the only thing we could predict with any accuracy were our costs. Avoid the fancy office space and the support staff and the guaranteed contracts. Focus like a hawk on your fixed costs and give yourselves a chance to succeed. Second," he continued, "you're about to discover that you have a lot of new friends you never had before. People will come out of the woodwork looking for a job or partnership opportunities. Don't let these things distract you from your clients."

A few months into our new venture, we would receive important advice from another Wall Street legend, Ed Hajim, who, even by the standards of other ridiculously successful Wall Street veterans, has had a career almost gaudy in its level of accomplishment. I still can't quite believe that he spent forty-five minutes on a milk crate eating a gyro and advising us about our business. The son of a single father who was often at sea in the merchant marine, Ed spent time in foster homes in the 1940s and early 1950s. He found another family of sorts at the University of Rochester where he majored in engineering and, as a recipient of a naval ROTC scholarship, spent three years in the Pacific after graduation. After a year in "plastics" he pursued his MBA at Harvard. He was among the first star portfolio managers of Capital Group in Los Angeles, the largest, most professional, and most prestigious money management firm in the world. From there he went on to manage the institutional brokerage business at E. F. Hutton and by age forty-one became a member of Lehman Brothers' board of directors. Wanting his own ship to captain, he became chairman of Furman Selz in 1983 and managed to sell the firm twice—first to Xerox at three times book value and then, after he bought it back at one times book, to ING in 1997. He has remained active with his own smaller investment funds and with a variety of philanthropic endeavors ever since, most especially his alma mater. The Edmund A. Hajim School of Engineering and Applied Sciences at the University of Rochester was made possible by a $30 million gift to the first family he ever had. Ed will be the first to tell you that a big part of his success was his willingness to share company stock with his colleagues to lash their fortunes together. This too is a lesson we've taken to heart at our company through the issuance of stock options. Whether it's one's alma mater, the armed forces, or any other group, Ed stressed to us the idea that all people have a basic need to feel as if they are part of a group larger than themselves. Now, as a member of our advisory board, Ed has told us that while a unified sense of purpose and pride isn't always easy to create on Wall Street, when you do, you're likely to be part of something special. The partners and I often remember fondly his first pep talk sitting on that milk crate in our first office.

Of all the frequently asked questions we get on the road— what inning are we in in the private equity game, how can you be bullish when profit margins are at all-time highs, and what are your thoughts on the twin deficits?—the one we've received the most when we started our little company had to do with the derivation of our company name, Strategas (pronounced stra-TEE-gus), and our logo, a centurion. Most people were kind in their questioning, but more than a few have been less than shy in their bewilderment. A master of nuance, Joe Kernen of CNBC said on the air, "Jason, you've been dreaming of starting your own company your whole life and this is what you came up with?" Similarly, a friend and paying client in Texas asked us bluntly: "What the fuck is a strategas, anyway?" I found the phrasing of the question so viscerally funny that I was able to experience, for the first time since I was about seven, the unique sensation of Dr Pepper coming out of my nose. The question also reminded me of my Georgetown days when, at the height of our basketball team's dominance, opposing fans would carry signs that read WHAT'S A HOYA?, or its more ribald and amusing derivative YOUR MOTHER'S

A HOYA. (The PATRICK EWING CAN'T READ THIS signs went over the line.)

Like most other would-be entrepreneurs on Wall Street we infused our decision to start our own firm with a self-importance that was completely inconsistent with its significance. As a result, we sought a name that had both meaning and the requisite combination of antiquity. The word "strategy" was derived from the Greek word *strategos,* which means "general." In Athenian democracy, the *strategoi* stood between the elected officials and its military leaders to provide counsel in balancing the needs of protecting individual liberties while at the same time providing for the overall security of the state. Ultimately, we decided, perhaps naïvely, that *strategos* was as good as we were going to get. As is their wont, however, our lawyers informed us that to name the firm Strategos could invite trademark litigation the day before we were to file. Having invested some time in the decision and becoming attached to the logo of the warrior we now affectionately call Gus, we asked our lawyers to find a letter that would complete the word "strateg_s" without inviting legal action. Essentially, we had to buy a vowel. They came up with "strategas," which, at that point, was close enough for us and turned out to be aesthetically more appealing in Greek lettering. There was a certain irony and sadness for me at the time that in our postindustrial and litigious society we had to choose a name devoid of meaning to steer clear of a lawsuit. Since then, the name has been both innocently and maliciously maligned and butchered. It's sometimes hard for people to take a firm seriously when they believe its name should be pronounced "straight gas." In any event, the name has been a source of amusement among our clients and friends. And, as the saying goes, "We don't care what you call us, as long as you call us."

And so we moved into a small conference room on the fifth floor of 780 Third Avenue, the five original members of our team cramped with computers and that infernal data board around a single conference table. The Trans-Lux ticker gave off so much light and heat that we often had to work with the lights off just to tolerate it. Over the course of the next eight months, we wound up cramming nine people around that conference table and our firm took on the physical and olfactory qualities of a DMV office in, let's say, Mogadishu. But, I'll tell ya. It was a lot of fun.

On our first day, I told my partners and our new colleagues that while we might fail, it would never be for lack of effort. During those early weeks of the company I bought a longshoreman's hook on eBay to keep on the desk in my office. What may have seemed like an odd decorating choice was actually a nod to my grandfather, Fiore DeSena, who had been a longshoreman on the Manhattan dockyards. I wanted to have a symbol, an immigrant's juju, of the great voyage we were about to undertake. I wanted to remind myself about a guy, probably not much different than I was except for the opportunities he was afforded, who spoke very little English yet came over from *la Campania* and swung that hook around and bought his own home and successfully raised eight kids. That hook remains a daily symbol for me of the Italian American experience. On good days, I look at it and think to myself, *Sic transit gloria.* Whatever we've achieved as a company could all be taken away in an instant. And on bad days, and there have been more than a few in the financial markets over the past few years, I look at that hook and think about how fortunate I am to work indoors with air-conditioning in the summer and heat in the winter.

I think about my heritage every day of my life and there is no question that the core values of the Italian immigrant experience have shaped the way I have approached my career and my decision to start my own business. Famed investor, client, and friend Larry Auriana is yet another example of someone who helped me—through our shared love for Italy and our ethnicity—when he didn't need to. We became friends almost by accident. In the summer of 2002, my wife called me excitedly into the family room to see a documentary on the dancing of the Giglio for the Feast of San Paolino di Nola titled *Heaven Touches Brooklyn in July*. The DeSenas hail from Nola, Italy, or more precisely Saviano, which is more or less the same town now, and it was remarkable to me that someone might make a film about a ritual I had heard about since I was a little boy. The film was so moving in its humanity and its depiction of the Italian American experience that I felt compelled to get in touch with its producer, Tony DeNonno. He told me that I too, as a grandson of Nola, could take part in East Harlem in the annual lifting of the Giglio di Sant'Antonio, a seven-story, two-ton papier-mâché statue, a practice that has its roots in Naples's environs. At the turn of the nineteenth century, East Harlem was the most densely populated urban neighborhood in the world, exceeding even the Lower East Side in human crowding, and it was the greatest congregation of Italian Americans in the country. I arrived at the appointed hour on a hot August day and ran into Larry. It was an improbable meeting that changed my life. It was improbable to me simply because Larry, after nearly forty years as one of Wall Street's most celebrated portfolio managers, had come a long way from the East Harlem neighborhood where he grew up. It was improbable to him because he never knew I was Italian.

The fact that he was there to honor his roots on that steamy day in what had become a tough neighborhood said a lot about the man. He could easily have been out racing one of the cars that make up perhaps the single most impressive stable of classic Italian automobiles in the world. But he was there on that day and what's more he appreciated the fact that I was there. Larry's father spent forty years supervising a hospital mail room, saving just enough money to send him to Catholic school and then Fordham. Eventually he partnered with the sometimes-flamboyant genius Hans Utsch, and although they had their share of anonymity and suffering at the beginning, they built their Kaufmann Fund into one of the most commercially successful mutual fund companies in history. (It has since been sold to Federated where the two still ply their trade successfully.) Larry exhibits an unpretentious intelligence that is hard to find on Wall Street, and although it's a cliché, it's obvious that he never forgot where he came from, his Italian heritage, his old East Harlem neighborhood, and his faith. He has made sure that I too will never forget the culture that lies at the heart of an impassioned way of life, replete with its ups, downs, and risks.

It wasn't the easiest of transitions to go from coddled Wall Street professional to entrepreneur. The transition was made even more difficult by the fact that I had lived in Manhattan for fifteen years, one of the greatest occupational hazards to understanding how the real world works. I didn't own an automobile until I was well into my thirties and although I had an extremely middle-class upbringing, the longer one spends on this island the harder it is to appreciate how people without expense accounts live. It takes great effort to not become spoiled and clueless.

The long hours and the anxiety associated with starting my own business, I learned quickly, became the wages of what had been previously a pretty cushy professional existence. Gone were the warm cashews and dry Cabernets of first class, the Carey cars driven by guys with mirrored sunglasses, and the obsequiousness of those catering to people like me who were, in truth, merely spending other people's money. Jim Moltz's exhortation to keep costs under control was always on my mind. On my first trip to visit clients, I learned to appreciate the all-you-can-eat breakfast at Embassy Suites. The stay revealed a fundamental truth about business travel—free booze and free breakfast is a powerful combination at $169 a night. The chain was owned and operated by Hilton Hotels and while I didn't purple light the bedspread, I was reasonably sure that the family's most famous offspring, Paris, would never be caught in one alive. The room was clean and comfortable, the service competent and unpretentious. Unfortunately, whatever positive afterglow I carried from the experience was quickly extinguished by the sole entertainment choice available to me in coach on my flight back to the Big Apple. As near as I could tell, I watched a bunch of half-naked people doing gymnastics at a luau for the better part of an hour. Only later did I learn that this was a Cirque du Soleil production and that many people found it entertaining.

In those first few years, my partners and I had to get accustomed to making significantly less money, to learning to navigate the shoals of balky technology and third world–style offices, to retaining all manner of accountants and lawyers, to satisfying regulators, and, if that weren't enough, to making sense of an intergalactic financial crisis. Still, it was the first time in my life when the great and romantic vision of America merged with my own hopes and dreams. As a patriotic small businessman, I needed no convincing of just how blessed I was to have been born in America. Still, I was surprised at the wonder of it all.

10

AMERICA, THE GREATEST SHOW ON EARTH

One of the great privileges of my job is that I am often asked to speak to our clients' clients, generally small businessmen and women and professionals who have spent lifetimes accumulating sizable sums through hard work and saving. Since the financial crisis nearly six years ago, audiences remain worried about the economy and their finances. Many are either in retirement or hope to be in retirement soon and they are deathly afraid of having the rug pulled out from under them just as they're about to cross the finish line. This is natural, but in recent years I've noticed that the questions have revealed something more—a deep and heartfelt concern, not just about the economy, but also about the country. And I have started to believe that this exposes the great and enduring potential of America: that people care almost as much about their country as they do about themselves. The media's oversized influence on our ability to process a constant barrage of news, most of it bad and disconcerting, makes it difficult for even the most steadfast and confident among us to maintain perspective when the market starts to fall. As legendary journalist Eric Sevareid pointed out nearly fifty years ago: "The biggest big business in America is not steel, automobiles, or television. It is the manufacture, refinement, and distribution of anxiety."

There are, to be frank, good reasons to worry. After all, if economics could be reduced simply to having central banks print money and having politicians spend it, there would be no need for a free enterprise system. Unfortunately, there are limits to the efficacy of monetary policy, and, as far as politicians go, it sadly sometimes seems as if Washington is where shame goes to die. Possessing the world's only true reserve currency, the United States can use deficit spending indefinitely to smooth out its business cycles. Europe has found out the hard way what Margaret Thatcher meant when she said that the principal problem with socialism was that sooner or later you run out of other people's money. Japan has had an enormous reservoir of internal savings to keep it afloat, but the country's demographics and xenophobia will make it hard to suspend the laws of financial physics forever. As it says in the Good Book, we know not the time or the hour.

While there may be no clear and present danger to the U.S. economy from its deficit spending and its mounting unfunded liabilities, the most serious and most difficult challenge for the country to address in terms of its future growth may simply be that six years after a financial crisis for the ages, the United States is still overwhelmingly and dangerously dependent on consumption and government spending. This is a problem when you're running a current account deficit. Gross domestic product, or GDP, is popularly defined as the sum of consumption, capital spending, government expenditures, and net exports, and many institutional investors and civilians alike are surprised to learn that nearly 70 percent of America's GDP is still dependent on consumer spending. The mass media generally throws around the heuristic that the consumer is responsible for about two-thirds of GDP. That is, indeed, roughly equivalent to the sixty-five-year average of 65 percent but it's a mile away, in dollar terms, from the current level of 68 percent. In an 18-trillion-dollar economy that difference is equivalent to nearly $540 billion *annually.**

Given all the economic and financial drama in the context of significantly higher unemployment over the past few years, our continued dependence on consumer spending may seem hard to fathom. This is until one considers how much G (government spending) was used to support C (consumption) in that time. Whether it was a tax credit for first-time homebuyers, cash for clunkers, or cash for caulkers, the Obama administration's solution was to prescribe as medicine largely what got us sick in the first place. Whether one believes that even more fiscal stimulus is necessary to forestall further economic pain, as Paul Krugman and other liberal commentators suggest, or whether one believes that the American consumer is long overdue for a crash financial diet, the stark reality is that history will likely view the debt ceiling debate that started in the summer of 2011 as the first salvo in a long and drawn-out existential battle for the heart and soul of the character of American capitalism.

At least for now, the odds of using fiscal policy to smooth out any future economic weakness are exceedingly long. While austerity has been somewhat discredited as a "growth" strategy, most fair-minded people aren't ready to throw good money after bad with more government spending, especially after the returns on President Obama's $780 billion "shovel-ready" fiscal stimulus package have been so meager and the costs of the Affordable Care Act remain unknown. Remembrances of the financial crisis will also make consumers less likely to spend, even if they could get

---

* Data as of 4Q, 2014.

greater access to credit. Without being able to rely on either C (consumption) or G (government spending), economic growth in the United States will be far more dependent on capital spending and exports (I and X) if it has any hope of growing at the same pace, about 3 percent in real terms, as Americans, and the rest of the world who exports to them, have become accustomed to.

There's nothing wrong with this of course. A greater emphasis on manufacturing, capital spending, and exports served us well in the decades immediately following the end of World War II. The problem now is that only 15 percent of our economy is in manufacturing and, unlike in the postwar period, our global competition is steep. Let's face it. It's easier for a victor to pay off its war debts when a good part of the world's productive capacity has been blown to bits. We have no such advantage now but, given the size of our debts and unfunded liabilities, growing our way out of our structural problems may be the only effective way of dealing with them.

The way America chooses to grow also has important implications for the social fabric of the nation. Regretfully, there is a yawning gap between the unemployment rates of those who are college educated and those who are not. The sad part is that in an economy that is 85 percent comprised of services, those lacking a college education find it hard to earn enough money to support a family without government assistance. At 2.9 percent, the unemployment rate for those with a college degree remains remarkably low. Those without a high school diploma, on the other hand, are nearly four times as likely to be unemployed and face an unemployment rate of 8.6 percent.* For some, such a discrepancy leads to a rather pat belief that everyone should pursue higher education. While this would be a consummation devoutly to be wished,

---

* Data as of December 2014. Source: Bureau of Labor Statistics.

it is simply unrealistic in a country of 320 million people. There are limits to how many people can become Web designers, or work in venture capital, or structure CDOs, or occupy the ranks of management—or even go to college at all. Maintaining a large and vibrant middle class was less of an issue forty years ago when people who didn't get a college education could earn a nice living in manufacturing. As many of these activities were offshored, many of these same people could work in the trades supporting housing in the eighties, nineties, and the first decade of the new millennium. Unfortunately, as it stands now, there is no natural industry to soak up such a large population of potential workers. This is why the country's recovery has been so muted and the unemployment rate has stayed so sustainably above what economists would consider "full employment."*

If history is any guide, it would suggest two potential approaches for policy makers, one cynical and potentially destructive, protectionism, the other more forward looking, the development of a new industry that gives the country a sustainable comparative advantage. While no one wants a trade war, it wouldn't be surprising to see protectionist sentiments on the rise. I would argue, even as a free market capitalist, this is so for good reason. It may seem like ancient history now but in the spring of 2011 Donald Trump became a political force for about two weeks when he suggested he might run for president. Whatever one thinks of the man, Mr. Trump has a not insignificant talent in recognizing what other people want, and at the time he recognized that most Americans believe in their own exceptionalism and were tired of the near-constant focus on the country's defects under the cloak

---

* The concept of what level exactly constitutes "full employment" is extraordinarily controversial in academic circles. The OECD defines it as a range of 4 percent to 6.4 percent for the United States.

of *change*. More specifically, he simply and directly expressed a frustration among most Americans with being pushed around by countries like China and the many oil-producing nations in the Middle East that are (dare we say it?) inferior to America in their pursuit of economic freedom and human dignity. As the richest country on the planet, America can more easily be magnanimous and accept these differences (and the economic disadvantages to average Americans they create) when times are good, but they appear eminently nonsensical, almost traitorous, when times are bad.

Although the Donald never quite expressed it this way, his brief flirtation with a presidential campaign exposed a simple, fundamental truth: allowing China to peg its currency to the dollar may be described as many things—practical, farsighted, etc.—but it is demonstrably not an exercise in free trade. He, almost alone among modern politicians and pundits, had the courage to question whether the terms of trade we have established with China have been some Faustian bargain that provided a boon to large multinational corporations that have the resources to shift inputs around the globe with relative ease at the expense of many small businesses and high-paying, middle-class jobs for those without college degrees.

Hundreds of hollowed-out manufacturing towns and fractured lives in the Northeast and Midwest stand as monuments to the insistence of the political and intellectual elite that anything described as free trade is always and everywhere in the national interest. In a country with 320 million people, it simply isn't realistic to expect everyone to be part of the "modern" economy. As is almost always the case, the poor pay more. Increasingly, economic policies that favor large companies with political pull at the expense of small businesses that remain the backbone of American enterprise and employment are heightening the political tensions between the educated and the less educated, between the young and the old, and between those with accumulated wealth and those who have yet to achieve it. One might say these tensions have been ever present, but historians would be hard-pressed to find another example in recorded economic history of such a rapid, willing, and vast transfer of wealth.

There is no denying that throughout time growing protectionist sentiments are often and correctly seen as the last refuge for politicians unwilling or unable to face up to the escalating costs of their own fiscal and monetary munificence. When it comes to the present period in global economic development, however, social scientists may find it almost mystifying that there hasn't been more debate in the public square about the potential costs of America's current "free trade" system. While this may be attributable to the fact that the benefits of globalization are a protected intellectual orthodoxy of the intelligentsia, of big business, and of the political elite, one doesn't need to be overly cynical to believe another politician may pick up on the political popularity of protectionism because this time it has some merit.

The other path to dealing with the country's fiscal problems, and a much better alternative to protectionism, would be to develop another new industry that would make America so productive and self-sufficient that it could pay off its debts by economic growth alone. There is potentially no shortage of candidates but the most obvious would be to take advantage of the vast natural resources with which America has been blessed. While some people insist for some strange reason on worrying about it, last autumn's big decline in energy prices is an unalloyed positive for our consumption-driven economy. With natural gas prices hovering around four dollars in the United States and LNG (liquefied natural gas) prices at fourteen dollars in the world's third-largest economy, Japan, the market's invisible hand is screaming for domestic production of natural gas for export. While the United States has fewer than 22 billion barrels of proved reserves (only about 2 percent of the world's total), the Department of Energy has estimated that nearly 400 billion barrels are recoverable using existing technologies. Of course, drilling can be controversial and there are environmental concerns that must be balanced with the desire for economic growth. Greatly exploiting our natural resources to create a vibrant export industry for fossil fuels solves many of the country's ills: it is immediately positive for our balance of trade and is thus an unalloyed boost to GDP; it is also a smokestack industry (without smokestacks) that can employ a lot of people and help to restore the middle class; and, last but perhaps just as important, it will stop us from enriching a variety of countries that may not have our best interests at heart. Perhaps it's too easy to put it this way, but beggars can't be choosers. We're broke and a true "all-of-the-above" approach seems both economically desirable and politically expedient.

These days it's not easy to watch the news or pick up a newspaper in America and feel sanguine about its prospects. Still, it's important for those of us who have a proclivity for the melancholy to remember two things: first, there are actually good people who wake up every day and try to prove the pessimists wrong; and second, there are probably more people like this in this country than in any other place on earth. I have been fortunate in my life to deal with a limited number of politicians, so I am hardly an expert about politics. Still, the one thread that seems to tie politicians of all proclivities together is their hopeless addiction to remaining politicians. One could only presume that this need just grows stronger the more prestigious one's political station is. In short, it seems folly to assume that President Obama is incapable of crafting this "grand deal" on entitlement reform that could tack two or three multiple points on the S&P in a heartbeat. This is not to say that it is likely. The head of Strategas's Washington office, Dan Clifton, would put the likelihood of such a deal at 20 percent in the president's second term. The point is that the market is placing the odds at zero. Black swans can, every once in a while, be good things. A nation disgusted with politics and the highly partisan nature of our national discourse can forget that. Good things sometimes take time.

It would be dangerous for economic forecasters and political scientists to extrapolate fully the Republican victory in the mid-term elections as a mandate for more limited government. After all, many Republicans seem not to be all that opposed to budget deficits either, if it suits them or their constituencies. But there seems to be, at the margin, a growing trend for taxpayers to expect value for their tax dollars, and to expect their public servants to have a greater interest in the public welfare than in establishing a long and lucrative retirement. California's Proposition 13 in 1978 showed that miracles can come true. In what many believe to have been an important harbinger for Ronald Reagan's victory in 1980, Howard Jarvis and Paul Gann convinced Golden Staters, increasingly alarmed at the prospects of having to sell their homes to simply pay their property taxes, to write into law limits on the ability of municipalities to levy ever-increasing assessments on homeowners. Proposition 13 is still extraordinarily controversial in California although most concede that it was one of the first important battles in the taxpayer revolt movement. Political developments in states like Wisconsin in recent years may give some indication of the general electorate's desire for reform. One hopes this spurs the animal spirits that have been the basis of our economy from the beginning. If companies could only be assured that they have seen the zenith of the uncertainty surrounding capital formation, they might start to regain enough confidence to make long-term plans to turn their vast cash hoards into capital that is productive.

While some tend to think that money and capital are equally interchangeable terms, they are demonstrably not the same thing. A quick textbook definition might put it this way: Capital comprises the physical and nonphysical assets (such as education and skills) used in making goods and services. Money is primarily a means of exchanging one good for another. Capital is measured in monetary terms, and since money (cash) buys physical assets (for example, buys a factory), capital is often thought of as money. But strictly speaking, they are different concepts. Said another way, capital involves risk and creates jobs. Accumulating money on the balance sheets of large corporations does not. One of the main reasons the United States was able to engineer unemployment rates of below 4 percent and 5 percent while Europe, even when everything is humming, can hardly get out of its own way has been the vibrancy of America's entrepreneurial class. Historically, job creation in the United States has been driven not by very large businesses but by small businesses that often rely on home equity lines of credit to get started and to expand. Greatly reducing the supply of unsold real estate and also creating some sense of certainty about the regulatory and tax environment might go a long way in bringing the unemployment rate down.

"So what's your solution, big shot?" It's a question I get in various forms when I'm on the road. It has not been uncommon for me, during periods of economic and financial stress, to go to bed and stare at the ceiling and wonder wistfully about the future of our great republic. Spending nine hours a day talking about the potential impact on the stock market of the country's economic defects and its secular problems will do that to you. But it's at those times that I remember Sinatra saying, "I'm for whatever gets you through the night." For me, at this time, it's hard to be optimistic and think of the things we could do as a country to get us out of the fiscal mess we've built for ourselves. Of course, it is a supreme conceit to believe one could come up with a plan to a seemingly intractable problem like the national debt. Still, there's something about an accumulated debt of $18 trillion that makes me feel as if I couldn't do much worse. What follows are five modest proposals that just might help America regain its rightful place as the world's economic engine. Some are more politically toxic than others, but as they say, there are few atheists in foxholes. Drastic measures are called for.

1. Cut taxes on repatriated profits. One of the great ironies of the country's current economic difficulties is that the balance sheets of companies in the United States may never have been stronger. As measured by the Fed's flow of funds accounts, cash as a percentage of assets and undistributed corporate profits for nonfinancial corporations are at all-time highs. The problem is that there is a certain sense in which capital is on strike, not in a conspiratorial Ayn Rand kind of way, but simply because few people like to play games, especially for money, in which it appears the rules can change capriciously. Companies appear to have little preference as to how they distribute the cash they want to part with; levels of M&A activity, dividend increases, and share repurchases are all listless. Some have actually suggested that it would be wise to tax retained earnings as a disincentive to companies to "hoard" cash. I'd like to go out on a limb here and say that if enacted, such a proposal would almost surely land itself in the pantheon of the World's All-Time Dumbest Ideas—right up there with New Coke and Lego fruit-flavored snacks. We humbly suggest a different approach—a reprise of the 2005 tax cut on offshore profits if used for capital spending, employment, or even, ye gods, dividends. Such a move would not only cut the deficit with funds unlikely to reach American shores but would also provide a boost to the domestic economy.

2. Auction U.S. citizenship. There are two methods for rationalizing high sovereign debt levels—cutting expenditures or raising tax revenues. Perhaps it's too pessimistic to assume that widespread spending cuts (actual cuts, not cuts in the rate of growth) are in the offing. That leaves revenues and, consequently, the two standard ways of increasing them—raising taxes or expanding the tax base. While it might be tempting to believe that higher taxes, in and of themselves, could put a dent in the deficit, empirical evidence suggests that tax revenues as a percentage of GDP remain remarkably stable whatever the tax rate. Put simply, tax compliance goes down as tax rates go up. Expanding the tax base in the modern age is no easy trick. Prior to 1945, armed conflict was a standard part of the economic playbook for countries that found themselves fiscally overextended. It was very Roman, in a sense, to find another land to conquer—and by extension another unwilling group of taxpayers—when money ran out at home. This is rather frowned on today, especially among democracies, and so that leaves legal immigration as the only sensible way to increase the number of taxpayers and taxes paid. Whatever its faults, America represents a promised land to millions (could it be billions?) of people seeking freedom and opportunity. Although it is at odds with our past and perhaps with our national conscience, auctioning off citizenship to the educated and the entrepreneurial—say $100,000 in general, $50,000 if you move to downtown Detroit for instance—could be a way to reduce the deficit while also bolstering the country's strong pioneering spirit. While this may seem like an odd policy prescription for someone who is the product of immigrants, I think it's important to remember that the immigrants who arrived in America in the early part of the twentieth century could count on no social safety net or public services. Perhaps not surprising given the fact that there was no federal income tax until 1913, even naturalized citizens couldn't rely on anything like unemployment insurance, Medicare, Medicaid, or Social Security.

3. Raise the retirement age or index Social Security to prices rather than wages. In terms of dollars paid, Social Security is the largest government program and represents the largest single expenditure in the federal budget, greater even than defense and Medicare/Medicaid. Anyone with even a rudimentary knowledge of arithmetic knows that as constructed the Social Security system is unsustainably solvent. When Social Security was initially signed into law in 1935, the life expectancy at birth of a white male in the United States was only sixty-one and in 1945 there were as many as 40 workers paying into the system for every beneficiary. Today the life expectancy at birth is over 77 and there are less than three workers for every retiree supporting it. That is to say, Social Security was never designed to be a lifestyle, but rather a benefit to those who really could no longer work and to their dependents. The program was almost immediately controversial and was blamed by some for the economy's relapse into recession in 1937. The first clue that there might be a flaw in the system appeared with the very first recipient of a Social Security check in 1940, a woman who lived to be one hundred years old. She collected nearly $23,000 over her lifetime despite having paid just $24.75 into the system. The Johnson administration's adoption of a "unified budget" in 1968 allowed the federal government to use excess Social Security funds for the general ledger, a practice that would land the average pension fund manager some quality time in the slammer. With an exceedingly large portion of people under forty-five not even expecting to receive any Social Security benefits at all, it wouldn't be all that politically costly to simply raise the retirement age for those more than twenty years away from retirement or to index Social

Security payments to prices, rather than to wages, to keep the system solvent.

4. Corporate tax reform and the adoption of a territorial tax system. Supply siders can be accused, just like Keynesians, of adopting a Johnny-one-note approach to economic growth, seeing tax cuts always and everywhere as a panacea for what ails the economy in the same way greater government spending and "investment" is relied on by the other side of the intellectual divide. Still, it would be hard for the intellectually honest to believe that a tax code of four million words could yield an elegant revenue-raising and capital-investment-inducing public policy. The corporate tax rate in the United States rests at a stunningly high 35 percent level—among the highest in the developed world. Despite this almost punitively high rate, tax receipts are remarkably low. In an era when corporate profits remain robust, it isn't surprising that there are quite a few progressives opposed to giving big bad businesses any further advantages. The critics of those wishing to lower the rate correctly claim that while the statutory rate is indeed higher than virtually any other place on earth, a variety of laws and loopholes means that no one pays it.

To my mind, this is precisely the point: the tax code has now become so cumbersome and convoluted that it only benefits those with the most creative accountants and lawyers. It encourages rent seeking on the part of American corporations, subverts the wisdom of the markets, and encourages American companies to keep hoards of cash overseas. The United States also appears out of step when it comes to its taxation of foreign-sourced profits. Most other countries have adopted a territorial tax system wherein firms pay taxes only on income earned at home. Current proposals would accomplish this by eliminating the taxes multinationals pay on dividends that foreign subsidiaries pay to U.S. parent companies net of foreign income tax credits. This at once would remove a significant disadvantage American firms now face relative to their foreign multinational competition. Combined with efforts to eliminate loopholes and make sure that firms pay their fair share, this simplification of the tax code would be broadly celebrated by both the business community and the markets. Perhaps even more important, it would likely raise more revenue for the federal government at a time when every penny counts.

5. Sell assets. When all else fails, the debtor goes to the pawnshop and sells the silverware. Admittedly, selling its stakes in Citigroup and General Motors didn't do too much to allow Uncle Sam to put too big a dent in America's massive debt burden. Still, the federal government has direct ownership of almost 650 million acres of land, nearly 30 percent of the country's total land area. A good portion of these lands is controlled by the U.S. military or is on Native American reservations. Still, much of it resides in the western states and sits on vast stores of natural resources. No one wants to see the Grand Canyon turn into a Six Flags, but these are desperate times, and some attempt to sell these assets, or at least to make them more available for commercial exploitation through leasing, can't hurt.

I have learned one thing in the eight years I've run this business: it's really all about incentives. Life and business are hard enough when the incentives are elegant and correct; you don't have a chance if you've got them wrong.

Milton Friedman remains one of my great heroes. I never met the man, but I was lucky enough to meet and become friends with another public figure just as passionate about the power of free markets to unshackle individuals from poverty. Larry Kudlow consistently supported my development as an economist and as a Wall Street professional as well as my thoughts on the way markets and the economy work. Perhaps we've gotten along so well because he too started his life as a Democrat. That seemed to change after he began his career on the open market desk of the Federal Reserve Bank of New York and, after a stint on Wall Street, became the associate director for economics and planning in the Office of Management and Budget (OMB) in the first Reagan administration. He really became a star when he rejoined Bear Stearns as its chief economist in 1987. His good looks and his eloquence in defending politically unpopular free market ideas also made him an almost instant media star at a time when the sum total of political commentary as we know it today was *The Mclaughlin Report*. He became just as successful in his second career as a journalist and has been a fixture on CNBC since *America Now* first began to air in November 2001. His eponymous show *The Kudlow Report* was a regular stop for those who intersect at the country's two major power centers—Washington and Wall Street. Larry was among the first to put me on television when I was starting out and was an important part of one of the greatest nights of my life, the gala for the sixty-sixth annual Columbus Day Parade. After a difficult period in his life, his commitment both to his Catholic faith and to his wife, Judy, have been an inspiration to me as I have tried to craft a career that could survive both adversity and occasional success. Perhaps most important is his almost infectious and undying sense of optimism about the country.

I developed a greater sense of his sunny outlook for America during my frequent trips to the Midwest and other parts of the country many large investment banks now largely ignore. These periods of euphoria for me are rarely reminiscent of Rousseau's— they rarely last more than two days—but they continue to lead me to believe more strongly in the idea that the world in general and our country in particular are becoming ever flatter and that that isn't a bad thing. The early morning flights from LaGuardia, the two-hour layovers and the connections through Chicago, and my Homeric odysseys to Kansas City through Des Moines, allow me time to catch up on my reading and to see the world as few who live in Manhattan do. When first faced with a three-hour drive across the plains without any real sleep and little chance of grabbing any, I felt hopeless, left with little other than my BlackBerry to keep me company. During that first trip, I called just about everyone I could think of in the first half hour—from my mom to the office (twice) to that left-handed shortstop on my American Legion team from 1983. I stopped short of calling my girlfriend from high school and eventually did something strange, at least for me: I looked out the window for a long stretch and actually thought about the places I had been in the course of the last week.

Although few might say that business trips to Hartford, Des Moines, and Kansas City were the equivalent to a trip on the Orient Express, they were undoubtedly more informative. Everyone knows that towns like Hartford and Des Moines have weathered some stormy seas. But if I had been paying more attention—as a strategist who runs a macroeconomic research firm—I would have realized sooner that not all of America's small towns are dying as the media might have you believe; in fact, some are prospering. Young professionals are moving into newly built condos in these cities and old industrial jobs are being replaced by new high-paying jobs in breakthrough technologies. Did you know that the unemployment rate in Bismarck, North Dakota, is 2.8 percent? Or that it's 4.3 percent in Des Moines?* These success stories are coming, to a certain extent, at the expense of cities

---

* Data as of December 2014. Source: Bureau of Labor Statistics.

like Detroit and Rochester, but they highlight the inherent dynamism of this country.

We have a long way to go before everyone enjoys the fruits of this bounty equally, but these trips often restore my faith in the strength of our economic system and in the power of economic freedom. As those cornfields and plains roll by, I reflect on the beauty of this country and more easily view and imbibe its pioneer spirit, its strength, and its sense of fairness. I think about the tough, no-nonsense yet unpretentious grilling I get from one of the country's premier mutual funds every time I visit Kansas City. I think about the receptionist who knows I will have little time to eat during my presentation and makes sure to wrap up a sandwich and a Coke for me for the long rides.

And I realized a long time ago that spending the majority of one's time on airplanes or in New York City or watching television is a good way to miss the essence of our country, and its fundamental goodness and strength. Last, I think about my dad and his vision of the country as a U.S. Army veteran and public school teacher. The country was different then, but he reserved his great ambitions for me and, while he was the product of a bygone era when one didn't take too many chances, I still try to make him proud although he has long since passed from this mortal coil. When I was about to enter my senior year of high school, my mom and dad saved up enough money to send me to a summer college session at Harvard. On a visit, my dad wrote a poem, "Summer Session,"* about his observations, and although I'm biased I think it's one of the most beautiful expressions of the wonder of America.

---

* Richard Trennert, "Summer Session," from *Holy Ground*, iUniverse, 2006, 68.

I walk through centuries of America:
Bay Colony buildings, The Federalist's,
Bullfinch Romanesque, Richard Georgian.

I watch my son disappear up the wide steps
Of Trumbauer's Widener library.
(Henry Elkins Widener perished on the Titanic *in 1912.)*

I sit back on the grass watching the silence of dusk.
I think about the humanity of scholarship is in studying others.

For a moment the great dream of America merges
with Harvard's and in spite of a proletarian instinct
Forbidding delusion, I believe no small
Collective pride went into the making of this place.

I cross Quincy Street, walk up Le Corbusier's pedestrian ramp
Delighting in all the work in progress of youth—
An eight-foot cardboard sculpture seen through tall glass.

I allow myself, as a father, a wish for my son:
Ride on the airy lightness of aspiration
But feel the solid weight of earth.

I exit on to Prescott Street.

The first time I read this poem, I felt blessed to be born here and sad that others didn't see my new vision of America as my own. While countries like France appear to have learned a different lesson from the recent near-death experience of the devolution of the euro by lowering the retirement age from sixty-two to sixty, the Steiger Amendment from the 1970s and union reform in the bluest of blue states today confirms that political miracles are still possible in America. While it is virtually impossible to imagine large groups of people in Rome or Athens or Madrid rallying to defend the benefits of limited government, there are still millions of Americans, lacking cynicism, who believe firmly in the founding principles of this country. Nearly 250 years after its birth, our volunteer armed forces are still willing to fight for these principles. The desire to deal with long-term structural problems before they metastasize into incurable ones is ultimately this country's great and unique strength. Despite its blemishes, the United States is still the greatest show on earth.

11

OTHER PEOPLE'S MONEY

Well, I spent six or seven years after high school trying to work myself up. Shipping clerk, salesman, business of one kind or another. And it's a measly manner of existence. To get on that subway on the hot mornings in summer. To devote your whole life to keeping stock, or making phone calls, or selling or buying. To suffer fifty weeks of the year for the sake of a two-week vacation, when all you really desire is to be outdoors, with your shirt off. And always to have to get ahead of the next fella. And still—that's how you build a future.

—ARTHUR MILLER, *Death of a Salesman* (Biff)

In a world where the media focuses almost endlessly and not without some justification on the misdeeds of our political and financial elite, one might wonder whether the traditional concept of the Wall Street customer's man—smart, self-effacing, and with an almost zealous commitment to putting his clients' needs before his own—has gone the way of straw hats, or, even worse, was merely some sort of nostalgic myth. But I know such men are not myths. My partners and I have been lucky enough to be taught by one of them—Jim Moltz, who gave us important advice about keeping a lid on fixed costs.

A product of Williams College and the University of Pennsylvania, Jim was hired as a securities analyst covering multiple industries at the legendary Wall Street research boutique C. J. Lawrence in the late 1950s. He rose to become its managing partner by the early 1970s, just in time for the entire industry to be turned upside down by the end of fixed commissions. As a result of this change, hundreds of Wall Street firms went out of business in those years. C. J. survived and even prospered by its strict adherence to keeping fixed costs low and hiring only the best analysts on Wall Street while other larger rivals like R. W. Pressprich and Co. and Auerbach, Pollak and Richardson failed. Stan Salvigsen, Charley Maxwell, Bob Raiff, and the aforementioned Ed Hyman all became huge stars in the 1980s at a smallish research boutique that once only catered to the institutional carriage trade. Jim Moltz remains one of the best examples of the fact that putting one's clients' interests first—being a fiduciary—is good business over the long term. Jim is also just a good guy. His perpetually bemused expression tells you immediately that he assumes the best in others and exudes the primary characteristic of class. He also makes everyone around him—from his fellow former board members at the New York Stock Exchange to the overly ambitious young strategist trying to make his way in the world—feel comfortable regardless of their circumstances or background.

In the aftermath of the financial crisis, guys like Jim seemed to be romantic anachronisms. More than a few people who loved the business and believed they were doing something good and honorable started to question whether the industry had lost its sense of honor.

"Who's running the real shell game here?" a friend of mine asked plaintively over a drink at the Campbell Apartment in Manhattan a year after Lehman failed. "Hedge funds who take twenty percent of the profits or the top management ranks of the big banks who routinely distribute fifty percent of the revenues in executive bonuses—with no high water mark?" It was, and remains, an insightful question and makes one wonder how Treasury Secretary Paulson could, only a few weeks after Bear's collapse, suggest with a straight face that the financial regulatory apparatus for hedge funds should look a lot more like what was in place for the nation's investment banks. Was this a point worth making, I wondered at the time, less than a month after a highly regulated financial institution got in so much trouble that the Fed was forced to use monetary tools last seen in the Depression?

Financial professionals aren't, as a rule, prone to navel-gazing of any sort. Wondering whether one's life has real meaning or where it might fit into the broader context of the cosmos, it is thought, is for the tree huggers who work at nonprofits and take their dogs to work. This collective identity crisis is due, in part, to the lasting image of the broker in the salad days of the 1980s—a swashbuckling instrument of capitalism who ate stress for breakfast and made everyone else not tough enough to work on Wall Street be just a little bit better. Hollywood has been all too willing to latch on to this caricature and has never really let go of it. (The next time you go to a romantic comedy, make sure to notice that the nice sensitive guy is an architect and the uncaring buffoon is an investment banker.) As someone who has devoted my life to the industry and likes to see its virtues as well as its vices, this saddens me no end. The potential remuneration on Wall Street will always make it a destination for those without a soul, bereft of character, and looking to make a quick buck. This characterization of the industry is so well entrenched these days that it even affects the guy in the back office who has to switch trains twice simply to be at his desk by 7:00 a.m. And more's the pity, because lost in the modern media's complete inability to see hues other than black and white is this glaringly monumental reality: the banking industry has been and will continue to be the lifeblood of our economy.

It is assumed that banks should simply be a means to store wealth and facilitate transactions. Virtually no attention is paid to the social utility of turning money into capital. Money is simply cash and, therefore, inert. Capital is the result of turning money into resources that one hopes become productive—a factory, machine tools, trucks, roads, and the like. The West's establishment of property rights and the banking system that has grown up around them turned assets into capital and fanciful ambitions into reality. As such, it can be argued that the genius of modern banking, while imperfect and subject at times to nefarious manipulation, has been the single greatest contributor to human progress, putting a serious dent in the crushing widespread poverty that was, even in Western civilizations, the norm rather than the exception before the modern banking system took hold. Academics have long noted the strong correlation between modern banking systems and national wealth, allowing businesses to take on more risks in their efforts to grow. Prudent risks can lead to faster economic growth, more jobs, and greater innovation in all fields of human endeavor. Of course the risks can be excessive, especially when you're a public company and have access to other people's money.

There have been more than a few times in the last few years, after the financial crisis seemed to change everything, when I really wondered how, a generation from now, when the books are written and some perspective has been gained through the passage of time, free markets, the single best arbiter of allocating scarce resources, could have gone so painfully awry. It became clear that one of the central ironies of the tragedy that unfolded during the crisis was that lightly regulated hedge funds came through the subprime mess far better than their more highly regulated sell-side counterparties. The difference in fortune stood as a metaphor for all that had changed on Wall Street. The net result of "a few bad apples" was a hastily conceived Leviathan of financial regulation that few of our legislators spent any time reading, much to the benefit of lawyers and accountants, and much to the detriment not only of the financial industry that might have deserved it but also of everyone else who can't pay for their ambitions in cash.

Why did hedge funds wind up being far better shock absorbers for the dislocations in the markets than their bulge bracket cousins? The answer, one might posit, lies in what economists would call the "agency problem," which like most academic appellations is simply a fancy way of stating a commonsense conclusion: people are far less careful about other people's dough than they are with their own. In the early 1970s, when the financial sector was only 6 percent of the market capitalization of the S&P 500 (it ballooned to 23 percent of the Index, and 33 percent of its profits by 2007), Donaldson, Lufkin and Jenrette's decision to become the first Wall Street firm to become public was seen as somewhat heretical. In many ways this can be seen as the start of the great divergence of Wall Street, financially and morally, from other professions like medicine and the law. Wall Street firms had always been run as private partnerships in which the reputations and fortunes of the partners were put on the line every day. It seems quaint now, but many old-timers wondered whether their firms could really serve two masters—a contemporaneous responsibility to outside shareholders and the solemn public trust of the nation's ability to raise both public and private capital. But by and by, those concerns fell by the wayside, especially with the introduction of negotiated commissions in 1975 and the growing popularity of modern financial innovations, like structured finance and other financial products.

One by one, all the great old firms took their opportunity to cash out and, in the process, gave themselves opportunities to use shareholders' money to produce asymmetrical payoffs through perverse incentives. Little by little, the concept of the grand old Wall Street firm died too and the notion of public responsibility was replaced with greed. Wall Street research suffered, now bought and paid for by investment banking departments, and the use of leverage skyrocketed, aided in large part by more muted business cycles and "the "great moderation." Agency fees, whereby brokers would earn commissions on the transactions of their customers, were replaced with principal transactions in which brokers would sometimes actively bet against the interests of these same customers.

This all became clear to us after we started our own firm. All of a sudden, after lengthy discussions with my partners about what we were spending on soda and coffee for the office in the early days (it still remains, by the way, mystifying), I wondered whether the partnership structure may be perhaps the single best risk-management system ever invented and whether hedge funds came through this crisis without creating undue systemic risk because most of the managers themselves had far more of their own capital on the line than the senior executives on the sell side. One feels sorry for the rank-and-file employees at Bear, Lehman, and dozens of other bulge bracket firms who lost fortunes big and small. But let's face it. The sympathy vote left town once people started to learn just how large and imprudent the risks were that some of these firms were taking. The fact that they were public companies acted as a powerful accelerant to the boom-and-bust credit cycles that are a normal part of free markets. Brokerage firm managers needed to keep up with their public company competition, regardless of the risks, and so they also elected to enrich themselves in the process. To be fair, a good part of this resulted from a mass illusion shared by everyone from Wall Street CEOs to the poor souls who thought they could really buy a house starting out with negative equity. The shared illusion was that financial "innovation" isn't always and everywhere simply another form of leverage, the lie we all tell ourselves when we believe we can get something for nothing. Management, shareholders, and consumers back then were happy when times were good but relatively few people are as happy now in the aftermath of the financial meltdown.

The public's outrage came to a head when others learned just how much Goldman Sachs had profited while everyone else had suffered. Impromptu picketing of the homes of Wall Street executives, some organized by motor coach, ensued. In early 2010, with the financial carnage of the 2008 crisis still fresh in the minds of everyone, the big questions facing not only Goldman but the public perception of the industry at large was whether Goldman would use their bounty to pay out the spoils on the deck of the greatest financial whaling ship of all time. The other smaller firms would take their cue from what Goldman elected to do. In an essay at the time, I described the scene this way: "It is nine o'clock in the evening and the brilliant reflections of Lower Manhattan's neoclassical buildings stream through the mahogany blinds of a gargantuan office on the twenty-ninth floor of 85 Broad. They illuminate, just barely, a middle-aged man with a balding pate. He is pacing, agonizing like a present-day Hamlet about what to do with an amount of money that gives new meaning to what is, unmistakably, an embarrassment of riches. An unlit cigar dangling from the right side of his mouth (he's no Jimmy Cayne after all), Lloyd Blankfein picks up a Goldman stress ball he picked up at a conference in Kiawah from his desk, nervously transferring it from hand to hand, and wonders, semiaudibly, to no one in particular, 'To bonus or not to bonus, that is the question.' "

The firm quite literally had more money than it knew what to do with. They had just posted earnings of nearly $5 billion for the final quarter of 2009. If it decided to pay its employees the customary 50 percent of its profits in compensation, the outcry from Washington and the media would have been overwhelming even for a bank that seems to take no uncertain pride in not caring what the hell anyone else thinks anyway. The country's unemployment rate was nearly 10 percent and the angry perception that the banking system was the root cause of the financial crisis was palpable. Unable to enjoy a bounty that would normally allow top executives at a publicly traded Wall Street firm to rest peacefully, the cash hoard engendered a nervous holiday season for Goldman's management committee. Senior management wrestled with an almost unanswerable question: how do we do what we normally do (i.e., take the money and run), when at best it would appear unseemly and at worst attract the ire of a restless and increasingly populist nation? While this was, to be sure, a high-class problem, it was no less a treacherous one.

There was of course a question of the optics of it all, especially when the country's top financial cops were looking for more scalps than Navajo Joe. Ultimately, Mr. Blankfein and his lieutenants took their cues from the political elite by devising a Rube Goldberg–like compensation scheme that simultaneously attempted to fool enough people into thinking they had satisfied both their top producers and the needs of the greater financial system. Paying out "only" $16.2 billion in bonuses despite a record year, the bonus pool was a mere 36 percent of revenue. If the pool had been spread evenly among all of the firm's thirty-two thousand employees at the time, each would have collected $498,000, a far cry from the $700,000 that some had predicted.* Of course,

---

* Graham Bowley, "Strong Year for Goldman, as It Trims Bonus Pool," *The New York Times*, January 22, 2010.

like all politically motivated decisions designed to have one's cake and eat it too, it fooled no one, making both the firm's stakeholders and the public at large unbearably self-righteous once bonuses were paid. The firm preemptively announced a $200 million donation to the company's education foundation, to mask its tortured Kabuki dance. The whole episode would have been hilarious if it weren't so hideously transparent and unnecessary. In free societies, good companies should have nothing to fear from their successes and charity should be accompanied not by cynicism but by genuine humanity and grace.

Austrian writer and satirist Karl Kraus once advised that in the "case of doubt, decide in favor of what is correct." And so, it would seem that the irony of Goldman's attempts "to suffer the slings and arrows" of their outrageous fortune gracefully could have resided in perhaps the most inherently capitalistic solution of all—distributing the year's windfall to the actual shareholders (formerly known as owners) of the company in the form of a special dividend. This would have provided an instant and not insignificant return to countless individual investors, pension plans, and endowments. Goldman's partners and its employees would have also received tax-advantaged compensation on the shares they already owned. And maybe, just maybe, it would have discouraged the vulgar mercenary culture that has surrounded investment banks since they abandoned their partnership structures and became public companies. But, alas, it wasn't to be. Of course there was the standard claim at the time that such a scheme would unnecessarily place the firm's "talent" (perhaps the most overused term in American English today) at risk of mass exodus. But given the zeitgeist at the time, the risk of such mass defections was low. It was an era when talent had been repriced. Intelligence, ambition, and a willingness to work hard are admirable qualities but were hardly in short supply at the time.

Hamlet reminds us that "conscience does make cowards of us all," and so I would be lying if I didn't say that I'm speaking about the crux of my own book here: I was a shareholder and, what's more, I have an intense interest in how our industry is perceived by the public. I met Mr. Blankfein only once, during an interview for a trading job when I was just coming out of business school. I remember only that he asked me about my SAT scores and then said—perhaps presciently given my career and his own current circumstance—that good salesmen rarely make good traders and good traders rarely make good salesmen. He turned out to be both and that may be the reason he got to be the head of the greatest moneymaking machine ever created. If he really does think he has been doing God's work as he has stated, albeit in jest, he should also believe as I do that our true rewards will come in the next life.

In the silliness that surrounded the Occupy Wall Street movement and the media's willingness to repeat the vapidities of the "movement's" organizers, it hasn't been hard to imagine that any number of Wall Street professionals have developed self-esteem problems over the last few years. Still, a fair number of those who work, literally and figuratively, on the corner of Broad and Wall probably don't care what anyone else thinks of their chosen profession and some may be proud of its raw dog-eat-dog image. What is most saddening to many of the rest of us is just how misunderstood the capital markets are in what is putatively the most capitalistic and free society on earth. The industry has no doubt contributed to this image through its own serial misdeeds and crimes. There is no sugarcoating these episodes, but it's hard to imagine that in a twenty-four-hour news cycle, no one seems to have the time to explore the historical importance of the banking system, the development of capital markets, and their contributions to the most rapid rise in the welfare of the common man ever witnessed in history. As a Catholic and sometime Mets fan, I am hopelessly relegated to being part of groups for which public derision is not only socially acceptable but actually encouraged in the popular culture. Again, some of this is deserved, but what is being missed is that Wall Street has been, can be, and will continue to be an important part of our economic and social development.

A dream factory of a different sort, Wall Street will forever attract young people seeking to make their way in the world and amass their fortunes. For the well connected, getting a job on the ever-expanding behemoth that is Wall Street has grown much easier, so it's not all that difficult to find a seat even when you're just starting out. It's much harder for those who don't know anyone to break in to the great game. But either way, what's really tough is surviving. Surviving the long hours—the travel, the venality of middle management, the siren song of dumb personal investments, and the ever-quickening pace of changes in global finance—with your health and character intact will not be easy. It will require a sense of humor and a perspective that usually develops only after some measure of suffering has been endured. My own struggles to get a job and to build a career on Wall Street have led me to believe that young people should consider the following advice:

1. Assume no one will help you until you've accomplished something. All the things you've heard about the large bulge bracket firms' mentorship programs and their concern for your career you will learn upon arrival are absurd. The "recruiting" process may have convinced you that you were highly sought after because your unique skills would allow you, in carefully measured steps, to climb the corporate ladder all the way to the C-suite. Sorry, folks: you're there to do a job that helps the firm make money, pure and simple. If you're unlucky, you'll run into someone who is purposefully trying to derail your career. If you're fortunate, people will leave you alone to privately pursue excellence. The chances are one in a million that someone will actively seek to help you before you've actually achieved something you've had to accomplish on your own. This isn't because people on Wall Street are mean-spirited, necessarily; it's because the pace and the stress of most Wall Street jobs leave precious little time for senior people to spare any meaningful time teaching and training those just starting out. This means that career advancement for the young Wall Street professional requires ambition, self-direction, and a thick skin. In a world where everyone these days gets a participation trophy, younger people are having a harder time realizing that no one will look out for their own interests better than they will.

2. Focus on achievement rather than status. The prudent man will apply a haircut of 50 percent to any outsized fairy tales of success and money heard around any bar frequented by financial professionals. In any industry largely made up of people of unparalleled competitiveness, it is natural to focus on beating the other guy at his own game. The trick is to figure out what your game is. Most young people on Wall Street care more about getting 21 and having other people know it than simply trying to beat the dealer. This is a recipe for perpetual dissatisfaction even when outsized compensation and status have been achieved. Learn to distinguish between pride and vanity. As Jane Austen pointed out, "Pride relates more to our opinion of ourselves, vanity to what we would have others think of us."

3. Learn to live the capital asset pricing model. A foundation of modern finance, the capital asset pricing model (CAPM) attempts to capture the relationship between risk and return. One half of the equation relates to the time value of money, the other half attempts to calculate the return needed to compensate an investor for the risk he's taking. As this relates to a career, the CAPM means, almost by definition, that those earning the highest returns will be the ones who take on the most risk. You may think you have it made because you made it into Morgan Stanley's two-year investment banking training program, but the highest earning member of your graduating class is much more likely to have taken the road less traveled with a company no one's ever heard of or have, ye gods, started his or her own business. A conventional Wall Street career can be both lucrative and satisfying but you should remember that there's a whole big world out there that doesn't care whether you made managing director. Some guy who started his own medical device company in the barn of his parents' farm in Des Moines will be able to buy and sell you ten times over.

4. Play to your strengths. This should be obvious for any well-educated, well-adjusted adult but it's amazing what can happen when you put a group of highly competitive people together in a survival-of-the-fittest type race to get a Wall Street job. When put in such a circumstance, normally rational people will abandon any thought about what they actually might enjoy doing or, even more important, what they might actually be good at when seeking a job in the financial industry. The focus often becomes getting a "better" job than the next guy, a position the mere mention of which conveys responsibility, wealth, and intelligence. Remember, however, that it's not easy to feel smart, wealthy, or important if you're in a job you're ill suited for in terms of skills or temperament. Tony Bennett is famous for saying that if you do what you love you never have to work a day in your life. Trust me, if you're good at what you do, the money will come. In an industry that isn't trying to cure cancer or put a man on the moon, attitude beats aptitude every time.

5. Realize that Wall Street is both large and small at the same time. This is less an issue today than it was when I was starting out a generation ago, but it is still common among most young people to assume that Wall Street is basically comprised of the largest money-center banks, mutual funds, and hedge funds. They don't realize that there are literally thousands of firms on Wall Street that might love to hire a bright and enterprising young man or woman who merely wants a chance. Success on Wall Street will always be largely a function of hard work, and of forming future, well-placed connections. Why slug it out among a nest of vipers at a name-brand firm when a smaller company might offer you the chance to make a difference and earn battlefield promotions? While the Street is large enough to accommodate a number of different career interests and paths to success, it should also be remembered that it is an insular industry, especially on the island of Manhattan. Don't make enemies. Take the high road. Be gracious in both success and defeat and remember that your treatment of all people great and small will be remembered, for better or for worse, forever.

6. Read. For the young person just starting out it's easy to forget, as it says in Ecclesiastes, that there is truly nothing new under the sun. Your ambitions, struggles, failures, anxieties, and successes have all been repeated millions of times in the four millennia of recorded human history. The quicker you realize you're not that special and that you've hit life's lottery by being born in a country where peace and freedom are considered givens, the quicker you'll develop the perspective needed to deal with the vast ironies of a life on Wall Street. We read to know that human beings are hopelessly predictable, to know that we're not alone, and to realize that the best and the worst of times don't last. Reading is essential to an understanding that investing will never be reduced to mathematical models, that it is and forever will be a social science. Most important, it should help you steer clear of trouble.

Last, everyone who seeks a job on Wall Street should have at least a passing familiarity with its social utility, of its vast potential to serve the economy, and of its ability to do good in the world. Then the money you make from year to year might not matter as much and, ironically, you might give yourself a greater chance of attaining and keeping wealth—albeit more slowly.

12

CONCLUSION–FOR THE LOVE OF THE GAME

Spoiled by material wealth that our forebears could never have imagined, many citizens of the modern world with all its conveniences, comforts, and opportunities nevertheless feel compelled to whine about absurdly trivial difficulties. The challenges for many of us on Wall Street are largely internally generated and often the result of trying to impress others while still maintaining some sense of ourselves, our individual traits, talents, and personalities—in other words, our souls. I try to remind myself every day just how lucky we all are, despite our problems, to work in the United States, the greatest republic in the history of history.

I wonder how often my grandfather came back to that railroad-style house in Gravesend, Brooklyn, and, after hanging his hook and his coat near the kitchen door, said to himself, "I'm tired. I don't think I can go on. I think I'll take a year off, write a book, and start my own firm." How often did my dad say, "I'm sick of teaching these dumb bastards *King Lear*. I'm going to go find myself." Fact: we all must play the ball as it lies. My grandfather had few choices, couldn't speak the language, and became, upon the death of my grandmother, a prodigious drinker. To be sure, my dad had more opportunities but, alas, he had the soul of a poet, and was ill suited by temperament and a need to tell the truth to enter the corporate world. Money wasn't that important to him and I'm sure that although he would never have admitted it he felt he was performing a public service.

Even after it became clear that our firm wasn't going to go bankrupt, I have remained cautious. The son of a poet, Italian and Catholic, I am superstitious to a fault and have a deep respect for the Fates. And as has become all too clear since 2008, we can never assume that success, once earned, is guaranteed to continue. If there has been a unifying theme in my life that I hope this book illuminates, it has been that every time I've gotten close to entering the gates of the City of Confidence, an anvil has fallen out of the sky to divert me to the Burg of Humility and Lowered Expectations.

Wall Street remains one of the most dynamic industries in the world. In some ways it is unrecognizable to me from when I started: mutual funds have been replaced by hedge funds as the Street's biggest customers, bulge bracket brokerage firms are acting less and less as agents and more and more as principals, and it appears that the sheer number of players and the democratization of information technology are making the investment world smaller and more efficient. My contrarian instincts tell me that it may be time for good lower-cost active managers to reassume their place in the sun after years of competitive pressures from hedge funds and ETFs. Through it all, a number of lessons have emerged that I hope will make my next two decades in this business (Lord willing) a little less dramatic:

1. Acting as a fiduciary is a competitive advantage. Before our first day in 2006, I asked Rob Kapito, president of Black-Rock, what advice he could give me on building a successful financial services firm. His answer was simple: "Put your clients first and the rest will take care of itself." It's a sad state of affairs when the concept of putting your clients' interests above your own is now so alien to so many in our industry that it has actually become a competitive advantage. Throughout our careers, my partners and I were blessed to have worked with many of old Wall Street's titans, who continue to cling to the Victorian notion that the capital markets perform a vital service for society, funding innovation, providing jobs, and raising the common man's standard of living. Sadly, the demise of the partnership structure seems to have changed all that. Most large sell-side firms appear to have completely abandoned their roles as fiduciaries and have come to see their clients not as long-term partners but simply as potential depositories of all manner of high-margin financial products. Far more than our unreliable ability to divine the future of the financial markets and the economy, our focus on simply trying, quickly and humbly, to serve the needs of our clients has been in retrospect the single biggest contributor to our survival.

2. The partnership structure is the best risk model ever invented. It may sound overly saccharine but as I look back over the life of our firm, it is clear that we wouldn't be anywhere near where we are today without a strong partnership structure. Nicholas Bohnsack, Don Rissmiller, and Dan Clifton have all become bona fide stars in the investment business and I think each one of us has been happy (and in my case relieved) to learn that we have complementary skills and emotional makeups. This has been extremely useful in our approach to creating timely and useful investment research but, perhaps more important, it has been critical in the management of our business. The last eight years have shown the partnership structure to be perhaps the single best risk management system yet conceived. Whatever the future may hold for us at Strategas, I will never waver from the idea that in business in general—and in an intellectual property businesses in particular—a strong equity culture is a good way to build on people's strengths while de-emphasizing their weaknesses. As the late Wall Street legend Tubby Burnham once said of his equity, "The more I give away, the more I make."

3. It's all about incentives. We knew when we started our company that the quality of our sales effort was going to be just as important as the quality of our research process. No product or service is good enough to sell itself, especially in an industry as hypercompetitive as financial services. However, we may have underappreciated how delicate a balance it sometimes is to create incentives that encourage growth and teamwork simultaneously. As an "economics" shop, the idea that you get what you incent should have been no surprise, but the extent to which we have found this to be true has been truly amazing. Get the incentives right, and the human spirit will amaze you in its ability to achieve heights previously thought to be unattainable. Get them wrong and human nature will similarly shock you in its ability to find almost incomprehensible ways to game the system. As a management team we are still learning that it is necessary to consider the secondary effects of our choices as intensely as we have focused on the initial decisions themselves.

4. Economics will always be a social science. If this financial crisis has taught us anything, it is that a blind faith in "mathematics" belies the nature of man. Wall Street firms can hire all the Ph.D.s in physics they want. They can create and rely on algorithms that would make Euclid himself weep at their elegance. But the movements of the economy and, by extension, of the financial markets will always lie outside the realm of what can

be expressed in quadratic equations. This is because economic decisions are made by human beings who are, at their core, social
animals whose strengths, weaknesses, foibles, and insecurities will
be most greatly exposed at times of intense stress. The failure of
Lehman Brothers and the financial crisis in the fall of 2008 demonstrated once and for all that concepts like VAR may "work" well
under relatively normal conditions but they will fail spectacularly
to offer sufficient protection in times of real trouble. An understanding of human behavior will always be a greater source of
alpha than a blind faith in mathematics.

**5. No matter where you work, someone's always worry-
ing.** I have found that for young people at large and established
firms, there is generally a certain confidence about the business
coming through the door that allows them the luxury of doing
their jobs without the anxiety of the firm's potential insol-
vency. While this might allow them to feel smug and may even
be good for morale, that sense of entitlement often produces behaviors in people geared more toward benefitting themselves than
the companies they work for. When you start your own shop, however, you realize that no matter what the size or competence of
the firm you work for, there's always someone worrying about the
firm's future and solvency. At small companies like ours, that in-
cludes just about everybody, but no one more than the partners
themselves. This runs the gamut from internecine battles about office space and titles, to cutthroat competition for our best people,
to perfunctory but time-consuming regulatory exams, and even to
burned-out light bulbs in the men's bathroom, Finally, among the
many lessons learned about Wall Street and business in today's flat
world is that the only thing you can count on is change and ever
greater levels of competition.

For all my failures and missteps along the way, I can say that

I've lived my life on Wall Street "all the way up," as Hemingway might say. It has been my passion and occupied the vast majority of my waking hours since I first entered a brokerage firm to cold-call midlevel executives and orthodontists when I was nineteen years old. It is a fascinating business and can be an extraordinarily lucrative one. The bigger payoff for me, though, has been the industry's power to fascinate, interest, and confound those who often have the biggest tendencies to overestimate their intelligence.

Wall Street was and remains a love affair for me. I have never had a full-time job in any other industry. I still love doing research that attempts to offer insights to professional investors. I still love hanging out with the traders and swapping dirty jokes. I love the pace and the characters and the game. Starting a new business has been an incredible ride—without a doubt the most challenging and intellectually stimulating period of my career. If it weren't for the existential threats to the system posed by the global financial crisis, I would also likely say that the last few years have been the most fun as well. Given the challenges the economy now faces, I can't say with confidence what my future and the future of my company hold. I do know that if we hold true to the principles of utility and humility we will have no need to paint the tape with our lives. Win or lose, we will be content knowing that our efforts reflected our character.

A QUIET NIGHT AT ROTHMANN'S— SEPTEMBER 11, 2013

I t's twelve years to the day after 9/11 and a week short of the fifth anniversary of the financial cataclysm set in motion by the collapse of Lehman.

Billy hits me on IM.

"Up for a pop?"

"Sure—where?"

"Let's go to Rothmann's. That's where I spent 9/11."

Although our crew visited "our bar" in a more desultory fashion than we did before the financial crisis was well under way, it was still like home. Pat Felitti, the gregarious maître d', had moved on to become director of Store Sales, Hospitality, and Operations at the legendary cigar shop Nat Sherman's on Forty-second Street. Artie the bartender had moved on as well, but Michael was still behind the bar. Brian, the intelligent hedge fund manager who seemed destined to appear as if he were perpetually a fraternity brother, was there although he had worked at two other hedge funds in the ensuing years. Jimmy, still enchanted by broads and sports, had plied his craft as a sales trader not at a bulge bracket firm as he did in 2008, but at an increasingly successful M&A boutique. I asked Pat Alwell, my friend and colleague for virtually my entire adult life, to come along and join us. He was quick to accept once he learned that Billy was, in all likelihood, going to pick up the check. One couldn't help but wonder whether Pat's success was in some way due to the fact that he still had his communion money under his mattress. While having a few drinks at Rothmann's wasn't a unique experience in the five years since I started to write these pages, the fact that it was 9/11 introduced a solemnity that rendered the proceedings more important than just any other night.

We raised a glass to our fallen Wall Street comrades, like my college friend Tom Galvin, who suffered at the hands of terrorists. And we also toasted, in almost prayerlike fashion, the well-being of some of our friends who had sacrificed their health, their wealth, and their marriages to a business that turned on them. Recognizing that, despite some of the hits we had all taken in the intervening years, we could all consider ourselves lucky. Strangely we all attempted to adopt an air of mature responsibility. The guys who usually drank the hard stuff drank beer and we *all* decided to leave earlier than we normally would to get home to the families that had stuck with us. In the cab on the way home, I thought that even at our advanced respective ages perhaps we were finally turning into men. Perhaps it was only natural, given the industry's transgressions, that both its sinners and its righteous stalwarts needed to suffer in equal measure for it to be granted some greater metaphysical absolution. In 2013 there was little doubt that we all had to work harder to achieve similar results if we were fortunate enough to have jobs at all. This was a good thing. Maybe we were at the point where we all realized that our true rewards might come in the next life.

I arrived home and had dinner with my wife and kids, telling them the story once again of my experiences on 9/11, remembering the city's collective sadness and attempting to suspend the memory of my friend Tom. I retired to my study after our pasta to read through a few e-mails and watch a little television. Earlier in the day, I had received a message from an earnest young woman in the Private Wealth department of Prestigious Broker Inc (PBI). It was the third time she solicited a meeting with me to demonstrate how her team "who have fifty years investment experience including forty-three years at PBI overseeing more than four billion dollars" for their high-net-worth clients could "help" me. She mentioned her experience helping the needy in Liberia and the fact that she, too, had attended Wharton. After her third entreaty, I wrote back:

> Ms. Efficient,
> I am currently very happy with my financial advisor who
> also happens to be my best friend from business school.
> With that proviso, if you'd still like to come and visit I'm
> sure I could find a half hour to chat.
>
> Jase

Although I now have my own office, I have never felt comfortable spending much of my time at any place other than with our salesmen and traders. I see how hard they work to attain new clients for my firm and, given my own struggles in the business, I have always tried to maintain a certain grace with those who strive. I've made thousands of cold calls in my career and still pitch new business at every opportunity. So I understood this young woman's perseverance and I gave in.

Ms. Efficient's response, regretfully, showed me that perhaps things hadn't changed on Wall Street as much as I had hoped or thought. Obviously whatever perspective and humanity she might have attained in sub-Saharan Africa had been obliterated by business school and her work at a large investment banking firm. Her offer of a meeting turned into a conference call along with a reminder that "we have quite high minimums here—ten million dollars of investible assets . . . to start a relationship." I had long ago been granted the wisdom to ignore the simple slights, humiliations, and degradations necessary to survive a life in the modern world. But on this night, of all nights, I couldn't help myself. I wanted to rage against an industry that insisted on ignoring its more noble roots in favor of a variety of behaviors that had gotten us into trouble in the first place. Before I had a chance to reconsider, I fired off my screed in an effort to score one for the good guys:

This is a remarkably irritating exchange and reminds me of why most people can't stand Wall Street in general and [PBI] in particular. I receive no psychic benefit from saying that I "work" with someone from [PBI]. You contacted me, obviously with a blast e-mail, and now seem to be worried about the fact that I might waste your time. You've only succeeded in confirming my worst suspicions of your firm and in establishing my solemn promise to myself that I will never work with it in any capacity. I don't know how old you are but I have suspicion that you are far younger than I am. Please do a little reading—perhaps even a little thinking—on what it means to be a fiduciary. Then reevaluate why you are in the business to begin with. Do you really love it—as I do—and see it as a long-term path to doing well for your clients and for yourself, or are you merely caught up in the idea that you work for [Prestigious Broker Inc.]?

Please, please, lose my e-mail address, Jason DeSena Trennert

The struggle to regain confidence lost, it seems, will continue.

AUTUMN 2014

Standing on a subway platform on a cold autumn afternoon, a guy slapped me on the back so hard I couldn't breathe.

"Jase, how are you doin', ya prick? What's it like in the one percent?"

I would have remembered that searing pain on my shoulder blades anywhere. It was Tommy from the floor.

"Tommy, what's cookin', man? How are ya? How's your dad? It's been so long."

"It's all good, man. Still livin' in Manhasset. Wife and kids are good and my dad is running with the same crew in Florida."

"What are you doing with yourself these days? What about Gene and Lou and the rest of the gang?"

Tommy shrugged his shoulders and grunted a little. "Well, Jase, everything changed after the Exchange went public. Dad sold out with a nice chunk but it was hard to make it work for the rest of us."

"I know. It's tough," I said sympathetically.

"The floor's a television set now. There's a Starbucks next to post 6 now. Can you fuckin' believe it? A Starbucks! It's a disgrace."

"Well, it was fun while it lasted."

"Yep, a lot more fun than selling software, I can tell ya that . . .
I guess money, eventually, changes everything."

"You're not kidding."

The 6 train approached.

"Well, here's my train. Take care of yourself, Tommy, will ya?"

"You bet. Let's get the crew back together at Rothmann's or
Charlie Palmer's or whatever the hell they're calling it these days.
Be good."

"Let's do it. That would be a lot of fun."

It was hard not to think wistfully about the old open-outcry
system on the floor that started under a buttonwood tree in Lower
Manhattan in 1792. Tommy was right. Sooner or later, money
changes everything. As it turned out, and in great irony, many of the
men that owed their livings to the floor turned on its most staunch
defender, Dick Grasso, in the end a reputational victim of his own
outsized pay package and an ambitious attorney general. Once he
was replaced and the New York Stock Exchange went public, the
romance and the humanity of the floor started to be dismantled
bit by bit by guys from Goldman who saw the old system not as
an important part of the social fabric of the city and the financial
markets, but just like any other business. In what is an intrinsic
part of capitalism, such a change could never have been avoided.
The old seats on the Big Board, once selling for was as much as $6
million in 1929 adjusted for inflation, were ultimately swapped for
$3.25 million in cash and stock as part of its transition from a car-
tel to a for-profit publicly traded company in 2005. The barber
was the first to go, followed in short order by the famed luncheon
club, an institution within an institution since 1898. Billions upon
billions of silicon chips replaced flesh and blood human beings.*

---

* At the peak of its influence there were 5,500 people who worked on the floor
of the New York Stock Exchange. Only 300 remain today.

GREAT WALL STREET BOOKS

The Money Game, **Adam Smith**

"Adam Smith" is a pseudonym for money manager George Goodman and *The Money Game* became an instant investment classic when it was first published in the late 1960s. The book offers an entertaining window into the culture of Wall Street when three-martini lunches were the norm and investment firms were still segregated among cultural and ethnic lines. Goodman perfectly captures the humor and ironies faced by a growing professional investor class tasked with what can seem a futile attempt to "beat the market." As the title of the book implies, running money management firms as businesses rather than as fiduciaries often involves treating investing more like a game than a long-term obligation to build wealth.

Free to Choose, **Milton and Rose Friedman**

Anyone looking for an accessible defense of free markets as perhaps the single greatest contributor to individual freedom and meaningful gains in the standard of living of ordinary human beings will find no better book than the Friedmans' *Free to Choose*.

The book was a companion publication to the ten-part television series on PBS exploring the efficacy of government policies toward inflation, free trade, regulation, and public education. Given the problems facing the global economy today, one could excuse the modern reader for thinking that this impassioned defense of free markets as a more efficient allocator of capital than the futile attempts of experts to centrally plan economies was written only yesterday. The television series also reveals Milton Friedman's brilliance as a happy warrior against the fallacy that greater amounts of public spending can solve all of the world's ills.

Where Are the Customers' Yachts?, Fred Schwed

None other than Michael Lewis himself has declared this to be the funniest book about the "lunacy at the heart of the investment business." First published in 1940 and accompanied by humorous illustrations, Schwed's classic takes unusual pleasure in poking fun at the various financial gurus and other costly experts who seem to be a perpetual feature of the investment business. Ultimately, the book reveals that human beings are almost shockingly predictable and that the more things change, the more they stay the same.

Once in Golconda, John Brooks

For aficionados of Wall Street prose, John Brooks may stand alone as perhaps the greatest writer on the financial industry ever. A longtime staff writer for *The New Yorker*, Brooks wrote three works of fiction and ten nonfiction books on business and finance. *Once in Golconda* is written with a novelist's flair for a story that examines the spectacular fall from grace of Richard Whitney, head of the New York Stock Exchange who, at his professional apex before the crash of 1929, would have been seen as the modern equivalent of a cross between Warren Buffett and Ben Bernanke. Sadly, he was revealed to have been embezzling funds from the NYSE's Gratuity Fund and from the New York Yacht Club, where he served as treasurer. He wound up spending three years behind bars in Sing Sing. Brooks brings Whitney's considerable gifts and faults to life in a true story stranger than fiction.

Manias, Panics, and Crashes, Charles Kindleberger

Generally regarded as one of the best investment books of all time, Kindleberger's masterpiece was among the first to eloquently reveal the predictability of speculative excesses and their consequent financial crises over two and a half centuries of financial history. The Ford Professor of Economics at MIT for thirty-three years should be considered the best and most prolific financial historian ever. After reading the book in the late 1990s in the midst of the dot-com bubble, I wrote to Kindleberger to thank him for such a generous contribution to the literature of the markets. He wrote back "on an old Royal [he] attacks with two fingers." His letter hangs in my office and is among my most prized possessions.

GREAT INVESTMENT BOOKS WORTH READING IN A TIME OF FINANCIAL CRISIS

The financial crisis and its attendant anxieties over the last five years led me to read the following books:

The Forgotten Man, Amity Shlaes

More than the standard hagiography of FDR and his economic policies, in this analytical gem Ms. Shlaes dares to wonder whether the New Deal did more to lengthen rather than shorten the Depression. It would be almost impossible to read her account of the Roosevelt administration's treatment of large and small businesses alike and not see some passing resemblance to today's regulatory environment.

The Lords of Finance, Liaquat Ahamed

As much as we'd all like to think that an invisible hand will turn the world's economic rudder in the right direction, Ahamed's book reminds us that economic circumstances are often shaped, at least in the short term, by all-too-human economic policy makers, with their own weaknesses, egos, and conceits.

The Mystery of Capital, Hernando de Soto
The esteemed Peruvian economist explores a central paradox: why does capitalism thrive in some countries and fail miserably in others? Drawing an important distinction between money and capital, de Soto believes title rights and a solid legal foundation are central to the capital formation process.

The Panic of 1907, Robert Bruner and Sean Carr
Perhaps even more interesting because it was written by Dean Bruner of one the country's best business schools, the University of Virginia, this erudite book is a highly readable account of a panic so great and dangerous that it led eventually to the formation of the Federal Reserve System in 1913. In the absence of a central bank, one shudders to think what the impact of this crisis might have been without the steady hand of J. P. Morgan.

Pictures of the Socialistic Future, Eugene Richter
Written nearly sixty years before any practical, real-time example of a socialistic society was evident, Richter's book and his ability in it to intuit almost perfectly a society based on equality of outcome rather than on equality of opportunity continues to amaze historians with its acuity. While a work of fiction, *Pictures* turned out to be remarkably prophetic.

This Time Is Different, Kenneth Rogoff and Carmen Reinhart
Somewhat more academic than the other tomes on this list, *This Time Is Different* became an instant classic in the study of what happens to societies in the aftermath of credit cycles that

occur with such regularity that one wonders whether it is futile to try to prevent them.

When Money Dies, Adam Fergusson

Perhaps the definitive work on the hyperinflation of Weimar Germany, Fergusson's history is insightful in poignantly depicting the impact that deficit spending and massive currency devaluation can have on a "developed" society's social fabric.

WALL STREET MOVIES WORTH WATCHING CLOSELY

Other People's Money

This film is perhaps the most unheralded, but most insightful, movie about the tensions between the responsibilities of a public company and the interests of investors and shareholders. The speeches at the end of the picture by New England Wire and Cable's CEO (played by Gregory Peck) and raider Larry "the Liquidator" Garfield (played by Danny DeVito) were shown to me during my first class in Corporate Finance at Wharton and I've never forgotten them. They should be required viewing or reading for any young person attempting to get a sense of what the true purpose of the capital markets really is.

Rogue Trader

A fast-paced movie that serves as a nonfictional depiction of a Bud Fox–type character in the form of Nick Leeson, a futures trader of working-class stock whose speculations destroyed Barings, an investment bank that had been around long enough to have funded the Louisiana Purchase. Ewan McGregor plays the ambitious but tragically flawed Leeson to perfection.

Working Girl

College-educated Melanie Griffith is terrific as Tess, a young woman from Staten Island subjected to the sexism and intellectual elitism that make it difficult for young women from the outer boroughs to escape the secretarial pool for jobs in the upper echelons of the brokerage industry. Sigourney Weaver is perfect as the upper-crust female executive who, while putatively Tess's savior, reveals herself to be just another cutthroat investment banker who will do anything to succeed.

Margin Call

This film may be the most realistic cinematic account of the stresses and deadly serious consequences of the financial crisis on the lives of flesh-and-blood employees of an investment bank on the verge of extinction. No book or movie so poignantly exposes the central dilemma facing Wall Street professionals at large bulge bracket firms: are my responsibilities greater to my clients or to the firm that signs my paychecks?

Wall Street

No list of Wall Street movies would be complete without this eponymous contribution to the genre. Gordon Gekko is a cartoon character of Wall Street excess, but Bud Fox illustrates perhaps better than any other the ambitions and *agonistes* of working-class kids striving to achieve wealth. Oliver Stone will never be known for nuance, but Fox's father (played by Martin Sheen) and the senior partner (played by Hal Holbrook) are welcome and fair examples that stand in contrast to the inherent cynicism about Wall Street depicted in the film.

ACKNOWLEDGMENTS

Ultimately, as in most industries, big breaks on Wall Street come only after ten or fifteen or twenty years of sustained effort and struggle. I have been extraordinarily lucky in my professional life because I have found, in time, people who genuinely cared about my career and helped me when I needed it. Throughout the text I mentioned Byron Wien, Ed Hyman, Ed Hajim, Larry Kudlow, Jim Moltz, and Larry Auriana. All of these men can be seen as obvious and one or two can be seen as controversial. But I've learned that anyone who's spent a lifetime doing anything of consequence will have their fans and their detractors, and all I can say is that these men have taught me, and continue to teach me, a variety of things I treasure about the financial markets, investing, management, and the responsibilities inherent in one's role as a fiduciary and as a decent human being.

A career in any field is dependent to a certain extent on luck. It is also dependent on having those rare individuals who take pity on you to help you out when you can offer little in return. Who was anybody, really, before someone gave him or her a chance? This is admittedly a short list and there are hundreds of other people I will forever be grateful to regardless of how my career turns out.

The one thing these men and women have all taught me is that we're in this thing together and that a random act as simple as a kind word of encouragement can have enormously large and unforeseen positive influences on another person's life.

No man is an island and so it has been with this book. My mother and father *always* put their ambitions for me ahead of their own and it's somewhat embarrassing to admit, at forty-six, that I still have my mom check my homework. I am also grateful for having friends willing to stand in the pocket when times got tough and the misplaced confidences and leaps of faith of a variety of bosses and market superstars throughout the years. The book you are holding in your hand is the result of twenty years of taking notes on hotel bar napkins and pondering the humor, pathos, and irony of a life on Wall Street in places as varied as Des Moines and Paris and Fort Wayne and Tokyo. Sculpting all of this material into something vaguely resembling a book required the incalculably precious time of my friends, family, and present and former colleagues. My business partners were extremely supportive of the project from the beginning. Nicholas Bohnsack, Don Rissmiller, and Dan Clifton are all bona fide stars in the investment business today and I will be forever thankful for their efforts in building the firm that has become Strategas.

My agent, Alexander Hoyt, saw the potential in this manuscript when few others did. He introduced me to famed writer and editor Ed Breslin whose advice and good counsel shaved off many of the original work's rough edges. It's not always easy to find highly literate people who are also good human beings and in that regard I hit the lottery when I was introduced to Alex and Ed.

Tim Bartlett and the gang at St. Martin's have been absolutely terrific to me. Tim and I may have different politics but he has an open mind and saw the potential of a book about not only Wall

Street's vices but also its virtues. Paula Cooper Hughes was especially helpful in helping me make the text tighter and also helping me "evolve." Thanks also to Claire Lampen, who answered my endlessly dopey questions.

My best friend from business school and my financial advisor, Steven Hadley, has seen the arc of a good part of this story firsthand and, upon review, added texture to my recollections of some of the events recounted here. He also made the wonderful suggestion to add the chapter, however painful, on 9/11.

There are a group of friends who can only be described as characters that contributed mightily to the content. I'd like to thank Mike Pizzi, Mike Liotti, Pat Alwell, Alan Goldman, Frank Chiodi, Stephanie Pomboy, Steve Duttenhofer, Paul Mastrorocco, Rodger Currie, Brian Toohey, John Barker, Jim Bankoff, Bobby Winters, John Crager, and Jay Coyle for all the laughs.

There were a number of people who supported Strategas before it was actually even a legal entity. Bobby DiFazio, Billy Heinzerling, Bobby Moore, and Rob Adrian saw the potential of the company when more than a few people in the business told us that we wouldn't last six months. Alexandra Preate is the CEO of what I believe to be the best public relations firm in New York, CapitalHQ. She is a great friend and has also been in our corner at Strategas from day one.

As one might suspect, a top-flight executive assistant was left to tie up many of the loose ends of the postproduction process. Deb Miller continues to create order out of the chaos of my daily life and I am again thankful. Strategas interns Sheelagh Coughlin and Justin Starvantino were helpful in proofreading various drafts.

Ultimately, most of the credit for this book goes to our clients— always the clients—men and women who take on the fiduciary responsibility of managing other people's money. Without them none of this would have been possible. A special thanks to Dean Dordevic for reading the book and encouraging me to publish it.

You may have noticed that *My Side of the Street* is dedicated to my lovely wife, Bevin. We met each other when we were twenty-four at a Mardi Gras party at Animal House on Eighty-second Street. I never quite appreciated how much of my bullshit she's had to endure over the past two decades until I started writing this book. A life on Wall Street can be a demanding mistress but it's never overshadowed the enduring love story of the family we've created together. A worrier by nature, I constantly fret about the future welfare of the other two great loves of my life—my son, Dominic, and my daughter, Marie. Thank you for enduring the absences and occasional vacant stares that afflict someone trying to write a book. Remember always that your character is your destiny. Never sin against the talents God has given you.

Thanks for making it this far. I'd like to sign off with one of my dad's favorite poems, a frequent source of encouragement during the lean times:

The Hound of Heaven, Francis Thompson

I fled Him, down the nights and down the days;
I fled Him, down the arches of the years;
I fled Him, down the labyrinthine ways
Of my own mind; and in the mist of tears
I hid from Him, and under running laughter.
Up vistaed hopes I sped;
And shot, precipitated,
Adown Titanic glooms of chasmèd fears,
From those strong Feet that followed, followed after.
But with unhurrying chase,

And unperturbèd pace,
Deliberate speed, majestic instancy,
They beat—and a Voice beat
More instant than the Feet—
All things betray thee, who betrayest Me . . .

INDEX